the OTHER GOD

Seeing God as He Really is

by Richard D. Exley

Logos International
Plainfield, New Jersey

Scripture quotations are taken from the Revised Standard Version of the Bible, unless noted as KJV (King James Version), TEV (Today's English Version), or TLB (The Living Bible).

THE OTHER GOD
Copyright © 1979 by Logos International
Library of Congress Catalog Card Number: 79-51902
International Standard Book Number: 0-88270-359-5
Logos International, Plainfield, New Jersey 07060

PRINTED IN THE UNITED STATES OF AMERICA

To:

Dick and Irene Exley, my godly parents, whose Christ-filled lives and unconditional love gave me the courage and the vision to seek for "the other God" and

To:

Don and Melba Exley, my brother and his wife, who have seen "the other God" and have become "holy lovers" taking His message to distant lands.

And once again a special word of thanks to Barbra Russell, whose typing excellence transformed pages and pages of messy handwritten script into a beautiful manuscript. A word of thanks is also due her husband, Jerry, and her son Dane who so willingly shared her for this time-consuming work.

Acknowledgments

Grateful acknowledgment is made for permission to quote from the following sources:

J.B. Phillips, *The New Testament in Modern English*, Revised Edition ©J.B. Phillips 1958, 1960, 1972. Used by permission of Macmillan Publishing Co., Inc. and Collins Publishers.

The Revised Standard Version of the Bible, copyrighted 1946, 1952, ©1971, 1973 by the Division of Christian Education of the National Council of the Churches of Christ in the U.S.A. Used by permission.

"Beautiful Dreamer" from *A Touch of Wonder* by Arthur Gordon. Copyright ©1974 by Fleming H. Revell Company. This material originally appeared in *Woman's Day*, a Fawcett Publication.

Who Goes There? by J. Wallace Hamilton. Copyright ©1958 by Fleming H. Revell Company. Used by permission.

Joni, by Joni Eareckson and Joe Musser. Copyright ©1976 by Joni Eareckson and Joe Musser. Used by permission.

The Hiding Place by Corrie ten Boom with John and Elizabeth Sherrill. Copyright ©1971. Published by Chosen Books, Inc. Used by permission.

A Bag of Noodles by Wally Armbruster ©1972 Concordia Publishing Houses. Used by permission.

Table
of
Contents

Foreword

What to read today is one of the biggest dilemmas faced by people who enjoy reading and desire expansion of their own thinking. With the press of time so keenly felt by most of us, investment in a book, which spells time as well as money, gets to be almost traumatic. Occasionally I am fortunate enough to have a friend whose opinion I value suggest a certain volume, so with anticipation I set forth to get a copy, feeling I won't be wasting resources.

Being a person who not only searches for content, but also longs for an engaging style to reinforce the material, I count it a privilege to recommend *The Other God* to all readers who also look for these qualifications.

Richard Exley's insight into the parables of Jesus are not only fresh and delightful to the mind, they become a tool to further understand the "unsearchable riches" contained in the Word of God. His colorful, forthright style makes the unfolding of truth a delightful experience. Knowing Richard well and being keenly aware that he has come to where he is through processes of sifting on one hand and being painfully forged on the anvil on the other, I only exult that the growth he has attained has enabled him to produce this book. And because he is a growing person, his future books will be somthing to look forward to.

Buy this book and find yourself caught up in love for this "other God" and the young man who tells us of Him.

Allen Groff

Introduction

It was about eleven o'clock on a Thursday night and Jim Calhoun and I were drinking coffee in the crowded coffee shop of the Writer's Manor in Denver. I was sharing with him my idea for this book because I valued and desired his thoughts on the subject. He did not disappoint me.

"Richard," he began, "someone once said the major purpose of preaching is to throw down idols. Idols are usually heavy and hard to topple and as you've already discovered, people don't take lightly to preachers 'meddling' with their sacred cows. What you are undertaking is not without risks. Still, I like it.

"The most difficult ideas to dislodge are not the obvious false gods of greed, materialism, or power. But a person's own inaccurate concepts of God. These they will defend obstinately!"

In the months since that conversation I've had reason to agree more and more fully with what Jim was saying, both the part about the throwing down of idols and about our personal images of God.

Spencer Marsh, in his book, *God, Man, and Archie Bunker,*

begins chapter one (appropriately titled, "Archie's God") this way: "In the beginning Archie created God in his own image, in his own image created he him.

"The major difference between this paraphrase and the original in the first chapter of Genesis is that God and man, in this case, Archie Bunker, have switched positions. It sounds weird, like the clay forming the potter, the bat swinging the batter, or the horn playing the blower. But strange as it sounds, the God of Archie Bunker was created by Archie in his own image. This God, who never existed before, even looks a bit like Archie."[1]

Archie is not unique in this sense, just more visible. All of us have done the same thing to a lesser or greater degree. We create a god with our tastes, our values and our goals. By doing so we have reinforced our prejudices with divine authority.

This book is about "the other God," the true God, the one many have yet to know. He may not be very popular, for He will challenge and confront the false gods we have created. He will call us to repentence and faith. He will move us to change and therefore we may resent Him, for old and comfortable ideas are hard to give up.

Some of you may think this book presumptuous, may feel that I am just pointing to a god created in my own image. I acknowledge that possibility and trust that such is not the case. The God I write about is not the god I grew up with, not the one I made in my own image. He came tumbling down and like Humpty Dumpty he couldn't be put back together again. "The other God" is the God of the New Testament, the heavenly Father as Jesus knew Him. He's a Father I've grown to know intimately, One who is constantly shaping my recalcitrant self to His image.

In the play "The Rain Maker," Lizzie, the daughter, speaks to a friend about her father, and says, "Some nights I am in the kitchen washing dishes, and Pop is playing poker with the boys. Well, I watch him real close, and at first I'll just see an ordinary, middle-aged man, not very interesting to look at. And then, minute by minute, I'll see little things I never saw before—good things and bad things, queer little habits I never noticed he had, ways of talking I'd never paid any mind to. Suddenly I know who he is, and I love him so much I could cry and I thank God I took time to see him real."[2]

That's how it is for me. (I started to write "was" but it's still happening so it must be "is.") When I finally stop rushing around, lay aside my prejudices, I see God real and I love Him so much I could cry.

I wish I could tell you what He's like. I can't. I am like the artist, William Morris, who was commissioned to paint June Burdow. He spent several hours before the canvas and finally showed it to her—and it was blank except for the words, "I cannot paint you, but I love you."[3]

I can't really make God known to you. These brief chapters are my best efforts, but God is beyond them, more real than they can ever be. Read them, not as a final word about God, but as invitations to take time to see Him as He really is.

Richard Exley

The Waiting Father
PART 1

And he said, "There was a man who had two sons; and the younger of them said to his father, 'Father, give me the share of property that falls to me.' And he divided his living between them. Not many days later, the younger son gathered all he had and took his journey into a far country, and there he squandered his property in loose living. And when he had spent everything, a great famine arose in that country, and he began to be in want. So he went and joined himself to one of the citizens of that country, who sent him into his fields to feed swine. And he would gladly have fed on the pods that the swine ate; and no one gave him anything. But when he came to himself he said, 'How many of my father's hired servants have bread enough and to spare, but I perish here with hunger! I will arise and go to my father, and I will say to him, "Father, I have sinned against heaven and before you; I am no longer worthy to be called your son; treat me as one of your hired servants." ' And he arose and came to his father. But while he was yet at a distance, his father saw him and had compassion, and ran and embraced him and kissed him. And the son said to him, 'Father, I have sinned against heaven and before you; I am no longer worthy to be called your son.' But the father said to his servants, 'Bring quickly the best robe, and put it on him; and put a ring on his hand, and shoes on his feet; and bring the fatted calf and kill it, and let us eat and make merry; for this my son was dead and is alive again; he was lost, and is found.' And they began to make merry.''

—Luke 15:11-24

M OST of us do not see life as it is but as we are. Our perceptions of people and events are colored by our feelings. Many, perhaps all, of our judgments are unconsciously biased by our own experiences—the pain of our present perplexity, the nostalgia of the past, the hopes and fears we have for the future. And so it is with our vision of God. Most often we do not see Him as He is but as we are; He is often nothing so much as the composite of our teachings and prejudices.

Much of Jesus' ministry was devoted to freeing men from these inaccurate images. His most frequently used medium was the parable. So much so, that Matthew writes, ". . . indeed he said nothing to them without a parable" (Matt. 13:34). Many of these earthy allegories were verbal sketches, word pictures of God as Christ knew Him.

Perhaps the most popular of them all is the masterpiece commonly called "The Parable of the Prodigal Son," a really misleading title because the hero of this story is not the wandering boy but the waiting father. With this truth in mind, I concur with the Scots who have entitled it "The Parable of the Waiting Father."

3

GOD AS FATHER

The quest for God is as old as mankind and continues ceaselessly even now. And out of this quest have grown the ideas which make up the creeds and faiths, the philosophies and religions of this world.

". . . Aristotle said, 'The Unmoved Mover.' Spencer said, 'Eternal Energy'—energy with a capital 'E.' Huxley said, 'The Unknown Absolute.' Arnold said, 'The Power not ourselves that makes for righteousness.' The Arabs, it is said, have a hundred names for God, and we in the western world have almost matched it. 'First Principle'—'Process of Integration'—'Cosmic Organism'—'Life Essence'— 'Fundamental Substance'—'Principle of Concretion'—'Divine Architect'—'Sum Total of Accumulated Idealism'—'Elan Vital'—'Life Force'—'Supreme Intelligence'—'Stream of Tendency'—'Judge'—'King'—'Almighty'—on and on, all the way up or down to the 'Big Boss' or the 'Man Upstairs.' "[1]

When Jesus came He said, "Father." With His verbal sketches He introduced us to our "heavenly father." A Father possessing the best of our earthly fathers—the self-sacrificing interest, the emotional involvement, the unconditional love—without any of their faults. A Father possessing all of their abilities but none of their limitations.

He taught us to pray, "Our Father who art in heaven . . ." (Matt. 6:9) and destroyed the kind of skepticism which prompted Mark Twain to sneer, "Special providence! The phrase nauseates me. God doesn't know that we are here and would not care if He did."[2] "Our Father" nullifies the kind of bitter atheism which caused Jean Paul Richter to say, ". . . We are orphans, you and I; every soul in this vast corpse trench of the universe is utterly alone."[3] Not the mere intellectual knowledge that Jesus called Him Father but that experience

---

[1] J. Wallace Hamilton, "Who Goes There," (Fleming H. Revell Co., Westwood, New Jersey n.d.), p. 13.
[2] Ibid, p. 13.
[3] Ibid, p. 13.

whereby His Spirit bears witness to our spirit and convinces us in the deepest sense that we are truly the children of God.

"Our Father" means God knows we are here and He cares, it means we are not alone, never alone! "Our Father" frees us from the inhibiting fears and superstitions which are the inevitable consequences of any other concept of God. "Our Father" gives us a sense of security. "Fear not, little flock, for it is your Father's good pleasure to give you the kingdom" (Luke 12:32).

Perhaps the worst disservice we can do God is to approach Him as if He couldn't be trusted to have our best interest at heart, as if He couldn't be expected to supply our needs without some exaggerated begging, as if He couldn't be depended upon to respond like a father. "If you then, who are evil, know how to give good gifts to your children, how much more will your Father who is in heaven give good things to those who ask him!" (Matt. 7:11).

It is not humility but distrust which makes us approach God as beggars rather than beloved children. God wants us to depend, not on our own worthiness, or our great faith, or even our spiritual ingenuity, but upon His eternal fatherhood. Remember, ". . . no good thing will he withhold from them that walk uprightly" (Ps. 84:11 KJV) and "Every good endowment and every perfect gift is from above, coming down from the father . . ." (James 1:17).

"Our Father" moves our faith out of the realm of abstract theology and into a personal relationship. We enter into a closeness and an intimacy with the Father which dispels the debilitating power of doubt, a closeness which engenders a trust that makes complete intellectual understanding and explanation unnecessary.

Still, in spite of all of that, there are those who rebel, who declare their personal independence and demand their inheritance, who take their journey into the far country, but even then the fatherhood of God is sufficient.

A FATHER WHO LOVES ENOUGH TO LET GO

The uniqueness and superiority of God's fatherhood is clearly seen in His relationship with mankind, especially those of us, like the prodigal, who are selfish and bent on having our own way. Jesus told this story, and He does nothing to glamorize the arrogance of this younger son. He allows us to overhear him say, ". . . I want my share of the estate now, instead of waiting until you die!" (Luke 15:12 TLB).

Nothing is said about the inevitable exchange which surely followed such a callous demand. We are only told that he divided his estate between the two sons. We can be certain the father did not try to use fear and guilt to manipulate him. Jesus said nothing about it, nor does the prodigal's later decision to repent and return home reflect any of the psychological barriers such tactics would have invariably created.

God responds to our rebelliousness by letting us go ("Not many days later, the younger son gathered all he had and took his journey into a far country . . ." [Luke 5:13]), not because our self-centeredness has made us unwelcome, but because it is the only hope for restoring the relationship.

Alan Paton has written a poem describing a father's anxiety as he witnesses his son growing up and leaving home. If this leaving, which is natural, produces such inner conflict, imagine how the prodigal's departure must have affected his father. Carry this one step farther and it's not too difficult to imagine God experiencing some of the same emotions as He witnesses our wanderings.

"I see my son is wearing long trousers, I tremble
    at this;
I see he goes forward confidently, he does not
    know so fully his own gentleness.
Go forward, eager and reverent child, see here
    I begin to take my hands away from you,
I shall see you walk careless on the edges of the
    precipice, but if you wish you shall hear no
    word come out of me;
My whole soul will be sick with apprehension, but
    I shall not disobey you.
Life sees you coming, she sees you come with
    assurance towards her,
She lies in wait for you, she cannot but hurt you;
Go forward, go forward, I hold the bandages and
    ointments ready. . . ."[4]

God also loves us enough to leave us alone until we are desirous of His loving intervention. Undoubtedly, word of the famine in the far country reached the father's ears; perhaps he even received rumors concerning the rich foreigner who went broke and was now feeding swine. Still, he did not mass his resources and embark on a rescue mission. He did not because he knew an untimely and unwelcome intervention would only serve to create further alienation.

"And if you would go elsewhere and lie alone with
    your wounds, why I shall not intrude upon you,
If you would seek the help of some other person, I
    shall not come forcing myself upon you. . . ."[5]

That is not to say that God does not care or that He leaves us to

[4]Alan Paton, "I Hold The Bandages and Ointments Ready," quoted in Robert A. Raines, "Creative Brooding" (The Macmillan Co., New York, Collier-Macmillan Limited, London 1966), p. 20.
[5]Ibid, p. 20.

suffer the consequences of our rebelliousness without the possibility of divine intervention. Rather it means He has made provision for our willfulness and wanderings that He is near to forgive and restore when we are ready to receive Him.

Nor is it intended to imply that anyone else can heal our soul's dread diseases. It simply means God realizes that often we are not ready to accept His provision until we have exhausted all other possibilities. Knowing this, He waits patiently until we can receive Him.

The story is told of a little boy who didn't get his way so he decided to run away. After packing his things—a peanut butter and jelly sandwich, a rusty pocket knife with a broken blade, some marbles and a piece of string—he informed his father of his intentions.

His father bade him a solemn good-bye and stood in the doorway watching him square his shoulders and walk away. Once the little fellow entered the forest which surrounded the family's summer cabin the father slipped out and followed, unnoticed, at a distance.

The boy walked determinedly onward, hesitating only occasionally and then just to get his bearings. After about ten minutes he stopped and ate the insides of his peanut butter and jelly sandwich, leaving the crusts for the squirrels. He then resumed his journey at a much slower pace. Soon it started to get dark and he looked around in fear, lost, not knowing which way to go. Dejectedly, he sat down and started sobbing softly. After a bit his tear-stained face lit up with an idea. He stopped crying, wiped his nose on his shirt sleeve, and stood up and hollered, "Daddy!" as loud as he could. He waited a few seconds and called again.

His father, who had patiently followed him, being careful to stay out of sight, responded by walking into the clearing where his son stood. The boy did not seem at all surprised and said matter-of-factly, "Daddy, take me home, I'm tired."

The "Waiting Father" is always near. He does not make us prisoners of His presence by demanding we be aware of His nearness, but He is near nonetheless, and He waits, unseen, in the shadows, until we call.

A FATHER WHO FORGETS OUR FAILURES

The father's strategy (intuitive or planned) was well conceived. One day his straining eyes sighted a travel-worn figure approaching the house. Failure and famine had taken their toll, gone was the swaggering son and in his place was a traveler whose shoulders slumped from an unseen burden; a traveler exhausted from more than just his journey; a man, old beyond his years, terribly scarred on the inside, emotionally emaciated. To one of the servants or a childhood companion he would have probably gone unrecognized, but the father saw something of his own likeness and ran to greet him.

Jesus only gives us the highlights of this reunion. He mentions a feast resplendent with old friends, new clothes, music and dancing. One element is especially conspicuous by its absence—the third degree. Jesus says nothing about it nor is there anything in the emotional fabric of this story to suggest it might have happened subtly behind the scenes.

This narrative clearly maintains that the boy's homecoming was so welcome that the squandering of half an estate was of no consequence—at any rate, it was gone and there was nothing to be gained by delving into the humiliating details.

With our curiosity and cruelty we expect the boy to be interrogated. We mask our morbid motives by claiming we want to make sure he has learned his lesson. Besides, if he is to be the recipient of our mercy we have a right to know. The father has no such curiosity. He will eventually hear his son's confession, but not as an interrogator. He will "priest" his son—hear his confession as a means of freeing him from its awful weight.

There is another possibility, not even hinted at here: the possibility that the prodigal was so shamed he could not receive his father's forgiveness or enjoy his celebration. Surely this was not the case, but imagine the father's hurt and disappointment if it were. This possibility suggests itself because life has produced many very real prodigals who have returned to God but have continued to live as if they were not forgiven or restored. We do not do God a service when we continually flog ourselves with the memory of past sins. In so doing, we are rejecting His forgiveness and yielding ourselves as instruments of Satan who is ". . . the accuser of [the] brethren . . ." (Rev. 12:10).

There is a story, supposedly true, of a minister who dreamed he was at the judgment waiting to be judged. In his dream he became very apprehensive. An angel seeing his anxiety asked, "Is something bothering you?"

The minister replied, "I am remembering all of my sins."

"You are a believer, aren't you?" asked the angel.

"Oh, yes, for many years."

"Well, then," the angel continued, "you have nothing to be concerned about. God has buried your sins."

"Where?" asked the minister.

"God forgot!"

A FATHER WHO RESTORES US TO OUR FORMER PLACE

Imagine, if you can, the prodigal in the pigsty. Imprisoned by his poverty, engulfed with a sense of failure, eaten up with guilt, starving to the point of desiring the husks that the swine ate—in that condition the best he could hope for, the best he dared dream, was to be allowed to live as a servant in his father's house. Obviously, he knew something of his father's love—he had to risk coming home in his condition—but never in his wildest dreams did he imagine love great enough to receive him as the son he really was.

Most of us, like this prodigal, come to God (our waiting Father) so sick of our failures and nobodyness that we are just hoping to be allowed to live as a servant in His house. Like David of old we have decided we would ". . . rather be a door-keeper in the house of . . . God, than to dwell in the tents of wickedness" (Ps. 84:10 KJV). Like the penitent malefactor, the only prayer our trembling faith can form is ". . . Lord, remember me . . ." (Luke 23:42 KJV).

And in response to the apprehensive efforts we finally manage, we discover, not the rejection we feared, not the servanthood we dared hope for, but welcome and sonship with all of the accompanying celebrations!

God is a father who sees something of His own likeness in even the most sin-ravaged and responds accordingly.

And because you are sons, God has sent the Spirit of his Son into our hearts, crying, "Abba! Father!" So through God you are no longer a slave but a son, and if a son then an heir. (Gal. 4:6, 7)

Do not allow the welcome the prodigal received to minimize the anxiety and apprehension that accompanied his decision to return home. It took insatiable hunger and homesickness to give him the necessary combination of courage and desperation to decide, "I will arise and go to my father, and I will say to him, 'Father, I have sinned against heaven and before you; I am no longer worthy to be called your son; treat me as one of your hired servants' " (Luke 15:17-19).

His well-rehearsed confession was unnecessary. His father saw him at a distance and rushed to him, smothering his efforts at confession with exclamations of welcome. Through his tears and laughter the old man began shouting orders, "The calf we've been fattening, kill it. And you, get those new robes, bring the best one and don't forget to bring some new shoes too!"

The prodigal's reception symbolizes the kind of welcome and celebration of which every son is assured. Jesus promised, ". . . there will be more joy in heaven over one sinner who repents than over ninety-nine righteous persons who need no repentance" (Luke 15:7).

The prodigal received a new robe, "the best robe," symbolic of Christ's righteousness. Underneath there may have remained some scars, evidence of sin's destructive activity, but as far as the Father is concerned all of this is past and now it is all covered by "the best robe" (see 2 Corinthians 5:21).

There were shoes for his feet—only servants went barefooted—and a ring for his finger. Someone has suggested this was more than just a ring, it was a landowner's seal. If this is true, then we are not only witnessing great forgiveness but also an unparalleled trust. The father is putting his son's name back on the "joint checking account," allowing him, without proving himself, to again conduct business in the family name. No wonder the older brother was shocked and angry. It's one thing to forgive a man, but it's something else to trust him again. God does both!

New Life For Girls is one of the most successful drug-rehabilitation programs in the world. It was founded and is directed by Demi and Cookie Rodriquez. Both are ex-addicts whose pasts are filled with drug-related crimes, imprisonments, attempted suicides, and hospitalizations. They were both converted to Christ and delivered from drugs through the Teen Challenge ministry.

Five years ago they felt directed of God to begin a similar ministry for girls. They began with $154.00 and a dream, and now New Life For Girls has centers in Puerto Rico, New York, Chicago, Kansas, Arizona and California plus a New Life For Girls home in Pennsylvania which houses, ministers to, and trains eighty girls at a time, and is valued at more than a million dollars.

When they began their ministry they faced some very real opposition. There were those who felt that two ex-addicts couldn't be trusted with the responsibility of such a ministry. In the last five years they have more than proven themselves and the transformed lives of hundreds of girls who were former addicts more than validate their ministry.

The prodigal was restored to sonship. Demi and Cookie are being used of God and thousands of other sin-ravaged people have been forgiven, restored and anointed to serve. No one is beyond help if they will just arise and come to the "Waiting Father."

Bill Gaither expresses this hope so clearly:

"Something beautiful, something good
All my confusion He understood.
All I had to offer Him was brokenness and strife
But He made something beautiful of my life."[6]

---

[6]Bill Gaither, "Something Beautiful."

The Waiting Father
PART 2

Now his elder son was in the field; and as he came and drew near to the house, he heard music and dancing. And he called one of the servants and asked what this meant. And he said to him, "Your brother has come and your father has killed the fatted calf, because he has received him safe and sound." But he was angry and refused to go in. His father came out and entreated him, but he answered his father, "Lo, these many years I have served you, and I never disobeyed your command; yet you never gave me a kid, that I might make merry with my friends. But when this son of yours came, who has devoured your living with harlots, you killed for him the fatted calf!" And he said to him, "Son, you are always with me, and all that is mine is yours. It is fitting to make merry and be glad, for this your brother was dead, and is alive; he was lost, and is found."

—Luke 15:25-31

A S has been previously stated, the hero of this story is not the wandering boy but the waiting father—our heavenly Father. This does not mean we are to dismiss the sons from our consideration. To be certain, there are things to be learned about ourselves from both the one who went away and the one who stayed. But these are things we already know, things we've perhaps ignored, denied or buried, but truths already known nonetheless. Jesus puts the father front and center because there is so much we still have to learn about him, this waiting one.

The most obvious is his fatherhood. It seems such an apparent truth could hardly need repeating and yet this is one of the least appreciated facts of our faith. Perhaps some of our difficulty in accepting the fatherhood of God is related to our relationship with our earthly fathers or the inconsistencies in our own fatherly roles. For others the difficulty may center around their first concepts of God. Whatever the reason we are all paying the consequences in terms of anxiety, guilt, faithlessness and alienation.

"Said the Robin to the Sparrow,
'I should really like to know
Why these anxious human beings
rush around and worry so.'

"Said the Sparrow to the Robin,
'Friend, I think it must be
that they have no Heavenly Father
such as cares for you and me' "[1]

So simply said and yet so profoundly significant. The trouble with much of our faith is that it does not begin with God as our father, and any faith without a father is going to be hard pressed to sustain us in these difficult times. Consider then:

A FATHER WHO SHARES ALL

This parable opens with the younger son demanding his share of the inheritance. The father responds by dividing his estate between them. It closes with an unresolved conversation between the older son and the father. The older brother became angry when he discovered the celebration being given in honor of his returning brother, a rascal if ever there was one. He refused to join in and so we see the father going out and personally urging him.

The son argues angrily of the injustice of it all. He who has worked so faithfully has never even been given a goat to have a barbecue with his friends and yet this immoral and irresponsible rogue is given a full scale banquet when he, broke and unable to provide for himself, finally stumbles home.

The father replies in astonishment, "Son, thou art ever with me, and all that I have is thine" (Luke 15:31 KJV).

With the telling of this story Jesus is showing us God as a generous father who willingly shares everything He has with us, His children. The need for such a story is readily apparent when one considers the background of Jesus' first century listeners. They, with their Jewish concept of God, needed it. We, the

[1]Richard D. Exley, "The Painted Parable," (Vantage Press, New York, Washington, Atlanta, Hollywood, 1977), p. 110.

18

equally fascinated twentieth century listeners, shouldn't have such an obvious need because we have a spiritual heritage grounded in the ultimate generous father story: "For God so loved the world [His children, even those in the far country of sin] that he gave his only Son. . ." (John 3:16). Unfortunately, our need is no less than theirs.

Many of us, like the older brother, live without God's gifts, not because He hasn't given them, but because we haven't received them. We live in need because our unfinished faith does not see God as real or understand the full significance of His gift in Christ. Paul writes, "He who did not spare his own Son but gave him up for us all, will he not also give us all things with him?" (Rom. 8:32). That is to say, Christ was God's best gift and since He has already given Him, why wouldn't He give us every other needed gift? His generosity is eloquently expressed in the words of the "waiting father," ". . . all that I have is thine" (Luke 15:31 KJV).

Much of our inability to act upon this truth is directly related to our poor self-image. Often we don't feel we deserve God's gifts; consequently we have difficulty in believing in God's willingness to give them.

Consider again the gift of Christ.

When we were utterly helpless with no way of escape, Christ came at just the right time and died for us sinners who had no use for him. Even if we were good, we really wouldn't expect anyone to die for us, though, of course, that might be barely possible. But God showed his great love for us by sending Christ to die for us while we were still sinners. And since by his blood he did all of this for us sinners, how much more will he do for us now. . . . (Rom. 5:6-9 TLB)

19

God's grace and gifts are never given in reward for our efforts, but in response to our true spiritual needs.

It's sad to see the prodigal starving in the pigpen when his father had bread enough and to spare, but sadder still is the older brother living at home in the midst of plenty and doing without. It's painful to witness the emotional poverty and spiritual destruction of men without God, but even more painful is the sight of the believers fainting from spiritual malnutrition when God has freely provided more than enough.

The older brother lived in virtual poverty, not because of his father's tight-fistedness but because of his own unwillingness to ask. James puts the responsibility for spiritual lack directly on the believer, ". . . You do not have, because you do not ask" (James 4:2). Many of us never share in the Father's wealth because our misconception about His character and our own guilt-spawned insecurities combine to leave us tongue-tied, afraid to ask and not daring to believe.

God truly is a generous father who shares everything with His children. We do not do Him a service when we "humbly" do without. In fact, we hurt Him by living without experiencing the fullness of our sonship.

Perhaps the most appropriate response to His generosity is found in Hebrews 4:16: ". . . come boldly unto the throne of grace, [to]obtain mercy and find grace to help in time of need" (KJV). This boldness is based, not on our merit, but on the evidence of His faithfulness and fatherly love. We have no confidence in our own worthiness but great confidence in His eternal fatherhood. Our willingness to ask, like the prodigal's decision to return home, is an act of worship which compliments the character of God.

A FATHER WHO INSISTS WE RETAIN
THE RESPONSIBILITY FOR OUR ACTIONS

It was probably more insecurity than humility which prompted the prodigal to pray, ". . . [I] am no more worthy to be called thy son: make me as one of thy hired servants" (Luke 15:19 KJV).

He left for the far country with a sizable estate and due, at least in part, to his poor judgment and mismanagement ended up as a half-starved feeder of pigs. One cannot experience such a humiliating turn of events without suffering some damage to his self-confidence. Often such a failure leads to unhealthy and demoralizing introspection.

The Scriptures indicate the prodigal underwent something of this nature when they say, ". . . he came to himself. . ." (Luke 15:17). The phrasing suggests that prior to this awakening he was not himself, not in touch with reality. It implies his physical actions were merely mechanical while he lived inside himself in an orbit of destructive self-analysis. He returned to reality when he remembered the security of his father's house, and that ". . . my father's hired servants have bread enough and to spare. . ." (Luke 15:17).

His emotional need for security was at least equal to his physical need for bread and that, quite possibly, was the deciding factor in his decision to return home. Freedom, with its accompanying responsibilities and uncertainties, proved burdensome. Now he wanted structure and security, someone to make the decisions and tell him what to do.

His is not an unusual reaction; in fact, it is very typical. We seem anxious to find someone who will give us bread in exchange for our freedom, security in exchange for our independence. This need undoubtedly accounts for the appeal of extreme fundamentalism, especially in light of the bad experiences this country had with the extremes of permissiveness in the late sixties and early seventies. We seem to be saying (both politically and religiously), ''Less freedom and more security.''

There are many political and religious organizations which will eagerly take our freedom in exchange for a pseudo-security. But God will not do this. He insists on making us sons, on making us retain the responsibility for our actions and our decisions.

If the prodigal had been allowed to become a servant, then he could never become the man he was meant to be. Only by insisting he remain in a responsible position could his father be assured of his son's possible growth and maturity. Such action was risky, to be sure, for the boy might have been so immobilized by his failures that he could not make decisions. Additionally, his father's generosity might encourage him toward further foolishness. Still, God deals with us in this manner because it is the only way we can fulfill our potential personhood. He risks our failures in hopes of conforming us to the image of Christ.

This freedom, this responsibility, does not mean we are independent of God or that He is not involved in our lives. It simply means we are free to choose. When we make the right choice we grow as persons and God amplifies our efforts. When we make the wrong choice He is near to help us recover and is able, as we allow Him, to make even our mistakes part of productive growth. God will assist us, influence us, help us, but He will not make us servants with no will or responsibility of our own.

A friend of mine, who is a truck driver, was talking about his relationship with God in trucking terms. He said, ''For years I've been in the driver's seat of my life and I've just about beat the ole truck up. Every fender on it is bent. From now on I'm going to let God drive.''

I told him, ''God doesn't want to drive. In fact He won't. He wants to teach us to drive. He will map out our route, ride with us, help us, but we always must be the driver.''

THE OLDER SON'S IMAGE OF THE FATHER

Until now, we have been seeing the father through the eyes of Jesus. If we can, I would like for us to see him as his two sons saw him.

It might also be well to note that how one perceives God (represented by the father in this story) affects how he perceives himself. It's almost like the proverbial question, ''Which came first, the chicken or the egg?'' If one has a good self-image he probably sees God as a loving and generous heavenly Father. If one sees God as good and merciful, then he will undoubtedly see himself as the recipient of that love. By the same token, if one is constantly down on himself he will probably see God as the executioner of his self-imposed sentence and as long as he perceives God in this way he will probably continue to degrade and condemn himself.

The older brother was undoubtedly a victim of this latter syndrome. His obvious feelings of rejection and insecurity were derived from a misconception about his father and once derived they continued to reinforce his misconceptions, which in turn amplified his feelings of rejection and insecurity. He was trapped in a vicious and destructive cycle!

He misunderstood his father's love. He supposed it was conditional, something which had to be earned. Consequently, his life was reduced to a calculating, nervous, neurotic effort to merit that love. ''. . . 'Lo, these many years I have served you and I never disobeyed your command. . .' '' (Luke 15:29).

23

The image he had of himself was so poor he couldn't imagine being loved for who he was, apart from what he did. His inferiority was so deep that it blinded him to the love his father gave. He did not love himself so he could neither recognize or accept his father's love. He was a perfectionist trying to prove his self worth and he cast his father in the role of the perpetually disapproving judge.

My heart hurts for this older brother. I think I understand something of what he must have felt, for I spent several years seeing myself and God in much the same way. Freedom came for me when I was helped to understand that God's love was unconditional, that my supposed unworthiness was really an accusation against God. I was not so much saying, "I am unworthy of being loved" as I was saying, "You are incapable of loving me."

The turning point came when a Christian counselor instructed me to remember the worst thing I had ever done. After that dark deed was firmly fixed in my mind I was instructed to think of the most Christ-like act I had ever accomplished. He then told me God loved me in my act of sin just as much as He loved me when I was Christ-like. Somehow it got through to me, where I lived, and I realized God's unconditional love for me and for everyone.

This freed me from my self-centered preoccupation with perfection. If absolutely nothing I did or could ever do could make God love me less, then it must be equally true that nothing I could ever do could make God love me more. I no longer felt a need to measure up, but this did not result in careless indifferent living; rather, I was so alive to the Father's complete love that I discovered myself responding in Christ-like ways which were previously impossible for me.

Unfortunately, this parable does not even hint that older

brother might have come to such an understanding of his father's love. In fact, the ending only reveals further his deepening disillusionment. When his father unconditionally loves his unworthy brother he sees it, not as evidence that he too is loved just as he is, but as additional proof that he is the unloved son in his father's unfair act of favoritism. He cries bitterly, ". . . 'Lo, these many years I have served you and I never disobeyed your command; yet you never gave me a kid, that I might make merry with my friends. But when this son of yours came, who has devoured your living with harlots, you killed for him the fatted calf' " (Luke 15:29, 30).

To him, and ultimately to all of us who share his feelings, and face the emptiness and disappointment of our lives, the Father says, ". . . all that is mine is yours" (Luke 15:31).

The Scriptures repeatedly affirm God's generous impartiality. Matthew writes, ". . . he makes his sun rise on the evil and on the good, and sends rain on the just and on the unjust" (Matt. 5:45). Peter declares, ". . . Truly I perceive that God shows no partiality. . ." (Acts 10:34). James says, ". . . God gives generously and graciously to all" (James 1:5 TEV).

The problem is not a biased father but a proud, self-centered son, a son who lives in continual condemnation because his best efforts to earn his father's love are always found wanting. A son who is so busy keeping score that he misses his father's expressions of love. A son who in angry exasperation will not allow his father to love him.

If only he would stop looking at himself. If he would just make an effort to see his father real. If. . . .

THE YOUNGER SON'S VISION OF THE FATHER
I cannot read this parable without remembering a pastoral psychology class taught by Dr. Lucius Jones. Most of the

students were young men preparing for the ministry; the one exception was a pastor's wife in her late thirties. She seemed more interested in understanding herself and her children than in learning the academic criteria as it applied to the course. One afternoon, before Dr. Jones could begin his lecture, she asked, "Why does my seven-year-old son repeatedly tell me he hates me?"

"I'm quite sure I do not know," Dr. Jones answered in his deliberate, dry way, "but I can assure you that he is very secure in the family relationship or he would never risk saying that."

As rebellious as the prodigal's actions were they still underline his sense of security. He seemed to understand the place he had in his father's heart. Even as Dr. Jones passed over the question of motivation to affirm the son's security so Jesus chooses not to shed insight into the younger son's motives but zeros in on the relationship he had with his father.

Consider the contrast between this second son's comfortable confidence and his brother's constant effort to measure up. The older brother feels unworthy and unloved in spite of his perfect record (Luke 15:29), while the younger son feels loved at all times. The first son never had so much as a goat (Luke 15:29) because he was afraid to ask, while his brother asked for and received his entire inheritance. The younger brother could take his inheritance and leave because he was secure in his father's love. He knew he was loved, not for what he did, but because he was a son. He trusted the greatness of that love!

And it was this confidence in his father's love that finally brought him home. Fear could never do that. It would have killed him in the far country. Some may argue that "the fear of God" would have kept him home. Perhaps, for this is undoubtedly what kept the older brother there, but I think the father's heart hurt just as much for him, lost in his father's house, as for his brother lost in the far country. Fear does not produce sons, but slaves!

The greatest compliment this father ever received was his son's decision to come home. The boy understood his failures. He cried, ". . . I have sinned. . . . I am no longer worthy . . ." (Luke 15:18, 19). He knew he had no claim on his father's love or his father's provision. The courage to go home did not rest on his loveableness but on his father's lovingness.

Love does not minimize the seriousness of sin or the reality of failure, it simply gives us a place to go with it. Love welcomes, forgives, heals and restores. Love is the source of new beginnings. Love enables us to pray:

Father
I've sinned,
made some wrong decisions,
misused my talents.
Still,
abused talents
are nonetheless talents
which You can use.
Help me to love myself
and feel important
because Your love for me
has made me important to You.
Amen.

The prodigal's salvation lay in his knowledge of his father's heart. He knew he was loved and wanted regardless of his wanderings and wickedness. And it was this image of a "waiting father" which finally brought him to himself and to his father.

The love which brought him back also made him new. He left willful and independent, after saying ". . . give me . . ."

(Luke 15:12). He came back in repentance saying ". . . make me. . ." (Luke 15:19 KJV).

When we finally see God as real we too will throw ourselves on the greatness of his love praying, "Make me!" Then it is that we realize we can trust this love, that His way truly is best, that He desires only the highest good for us. We will hear Him say,

"All which I took from thee, I did but take,
   Not for thy harms,
But just that thou might'st seek it in My arms.
   All which thy child's mistake
Fancies as lost, I have stored for thee at home:
   Rise, clasp my hand, and come!"[2]

[2]Francis Thompson, "The Hound of Heaven," (Fleming H. Revell Co., Westwood, New Jersey, n.d.), p. 18.

The God Who Provides

And he said to them, "Which of you who has a friend will go to him at midnight and say to him, 'Friend, lend me three loaves; for a friend of mine has arrived on a journey, and I have nothing to set before him'; and he will answer from within, 'Do not bother me; the door is now shut, and my children are with me in bed; I cannot get up and give you anything'? I tell you, though he will not get up and give him anything because he is his friend, yet because of his importunity he will rise and give him whatever he needs. And I tell you, Ask, and it will be given you; seek, and you will find; knock, and it will be opened to you. For everyone who asks receives, and he who seeks finds, and to him who knocks it will be opened."

—Luke 11:5-10

And he told them a parable, to the effect that they ought always to pray and not lose heart. He said, "In a certain city there was a judge who neither feared God or regarded man; and there was a widow in that city who kept coming to him and saying, 'Vindicate me against my adversary.' For a while he refused; but afterward he said to himself, 'Though I neither fear

God nor regard man, yet because this widow bothers me, I will vindicate her, or she will wear me out by her continual coming.' '' And the Lord said, ''Hear what the unrighteous judge says. And will not God vindicate his elect, who cry to him day and night? Will he delay long over them? I tell you, he will vindicate them speedily. Nevertheless, when the Son of man comes, will he find faith on earth?''

—Luke 18:1-8

THESE two parables differ from most in that they are contrasts, not comparisons. In most of the parables depicting God, Christ used the main character as a God-type. Not so here. Luke's portrait of this unsympathetic friend bears no resemblence to the compassionate God whom Christ taught us to call Father. And the vain, obnoxious judge of Luke 18 is even less like the loving God Christ has made known to us. Both the friend and the judge are opposites of God, stark contrasts to Him.

Christ employs these two unsavory characters in much the same way a jeweler utilizes black velvet to display his diamonds to best advantage. Never is the character of God more appealing than when it is seen against the backdrop of these two dark, unfeeling men. Their cruelty seems only to emphasize His goodness.

These parables do not suggest, as some have mistakenly concluded, that God can be influenced or manipulated by stubborn, strong-willed prayers. That He does not need to be persuaded to bless us is declared in Luke 12:32: "Fear not, little flock, for it is your Father's good pleasure to give you the kingdom." Neither is the purpose of prayer to inform Him of our needs, ". . . for your Father knows what you need before you ask him" (Matt. 6:8). Christ is merely encouraging us to trust the goodness of God. If these two hard hearts can respond to human need, how dare we doubt the willingness of God!

WHEN LIFE GETS OUT OF HAND

Science and technology seem to have made many indifferent to the goodness of God. If men are capable of providing for themselves, if they have no need of God, why should they care whether He is compassionate or not? Yet, is anyone truly self-sufficient, truly independent of God? I think not.

The recent drought makes our dependence obvious. In the event of another drought we probably have enough resources stockpiled to survive for a time, but what if the drought continued on and on? Attempts at rain-making have proven to be largely unsuccessful and in truth we are dependent on God for even the rain that we need.

> "Back of the bread is the snowy flour
> And back of the flour the mill
> And back of the mill is the field of wheat
> The rain, and the Father's will."[1]

Conscientious preparation and careful management can reduce our vulnerability to circumstances, but inevitably life catches us unprepared. Sooner or later we find ourselves surprised by an unexpected demand. We awake to a pounding on our door, a familiar voice calls from the dark announcing an unexpected guest who is weary and hungry from his journey and we have nothing in the house to offer him.

Jesus knows how to tell a story and we all catch ourselves smiling and nodding in sympathy with the embarrassed host He speaks of. We've all been in his shoes—the house is messy, dinner dishes still on the table and the doorbell rings. Who

[1]Ray C. Stedman, "Jesus Teaches on Prayer," (Word Books, Waco, Texas 1975), p. 72. Used by permission of Word Books, Publisher. Waco, Texas.

hasn't had out-of-town guests drop in, unannounced, two days before payday?

Don't be fooled, this is more than just a story. It is life laid bare by the one who understands it best. He's warning us, telling us, that sooner or later life is going to surprise us with some unexpected demands. He does not hint as to what form they will take but experience suggests a number of possibilities: delinquency, divorce, a business failure, a crippling accident, a terminal illness, death? Not necessarily to us, but in ways that affect us.

This host provided because he was resourceful. He did not sit down and wring his hands in despair, he took action. Through the dark streets, through the narrow, unmarked alleys he journeys until he reaches, at last, a house familiar, even in the dark. He pounds on the door, he makes his situation known, he begs bread.

How did he know where to go? Why was he so sure this friend had bread? We can assume that he has been here before, that this is a familiar friend, one whose hospitality he has enjoyed on frequent occasions. Does he not remember his friend's table groaning beneath its burden of bread, his friend's cupboard about to burst with its abundance? This is no shot in the dark. It's a plea based on experience.

What will we do in the midnight of our need, when the light of life is gone, when our personal cupboards are despairingly bare?

Any conclusion here is speculation, to be sure, but let me suggest that a familiarity with prayer's pathway to God will increase one's ability to find Him in the darkness. If we have come often to God in the sunshine of our lives, our anxious feet will find the familiar pathway, even in the darkest night. Though blinded by disaster, though hounded and hindered by doubt, though confused by life which seems out of hand, we can find our way to God intuitively because going to Him has become second nature, a way of life.

With this in mind, I'm learning to pray:

"Lord,
Help me
to find You sufficient
in my recurring bouts
with hangnails
and other little hurts
so that I will know
where to find You
if life should hand me
some real heartaches.
Amen."[2]

GOD'S SUFFICIENCY

Confidence in God's willing goodness is necessary to a living faith, but alone it is not enough. We must also know His resources are sufficient to supply our most demanding need. His willingness is small comfort if He does not have the power to intervene triumphantly.

No serious Bible student can doubt God's sufficiency, for the Scriptures are filled with accounts of His abundant provision. When Adam and Eve sinned and became ashamed of their nakedness, God made them ". . . coats of skins and clothed them" (Gen. 3:21 KJV). Isaac asked his father, ". . . Behold the fire and the wood: but where is the lamb for a burnt offering?" (Gen. 22:7). Abraham answered, ". . . God will provide. . ." (Gen. 22:8) and He did with "a ram caught in a thicket by his horns. . ." (Gen. 22:13).

And this is only the beginning: Daily (with the exception of

[2]Richard D. Exley, "The Painted Parable," (Vantage Press, New York, Washington, Atlanta, Hollywood, 1977), p. 110.

the Sabbath) for forty years, He fed two million Israelites with bread from heaven and quenched their thirst with water from rocks. During an extended drought, ravens fed Elijah each morning and night. For an extended period God miraculously sustained a widow, her son and the prophet with an almost empty meal barrel and a small cruse of oil.

Christ turned water into wine, got tax money from a fish's mouth, fed thousands with the fragments of a small boy's lunch, calmed stormy seas, healed the sick, cleansed lepers, caused the blind to see, raised the dead and forgave sins! "For with God nothing will be impossible" (Luke 1:37).

God's provisions are not limited to our physical needs. He knows we cannot live by bread alone so he provides forgiveness for the guilty, salvation for the sinful, peace for the troubled, love for the lonely and friendless, rest for the weary, joy for the sorrowful, and strength for the weak. Paul declares, ". . . my God will supply every need of yours . . ." (Phil. 4:19). David writes, "I have been young and now am old; yet have I not seen the righteous forsaken, nor his seed begging bread" (Ps. 37:25 KJV). Christ promises, "My grace is sufficient for you. . ." (2 Cor. 12:9).

When life takes you by surprise, with some unexpected demands, do not be afraid, for God is not unprepared, ". . .he that keepeth thee will not slumber" (Ps. 121:3 KJV). When famine and poverty overtook the prodigal he said, ". . . [my father has] bread enough and to spare. . . . I will arise and go to [him] . . ." (Luke 15:17, 18).

The song writer said it well:

" 'Tis the grandest theme thro' the ages rung;
'Tis the grandest theme for a mortal tongue;
'Tis the grandest theme that the world e'er sung;

'Our God is able to deliver thee.'
He is able to deliver thee,
He is able to deliver thee,
Tho' by sin opprest, Go to Him for rest,
'Our God is able to deliver thee.' "[3]

Some years ago I visited the First Methodist Church in Houston, Texas, so I could hear Dr. Charles Allen preach. That morning he was preaching about prayer and the sufficiency of God and he told this story:

"The bishop was the guest speaker in a local Methodist church and following service he was conversing with several of the members. In the course of conversation he asked if they were pleased with their new pastor.

"There were several immediate answers of affirmation and one man, more outspoken than the rest said, 'Bishop, our new pastor asks God for things our old pastor never even knew He had!"

". . . God . . . is able to do far more than we would ever dare to ask or even dream of—infinitely beyond our highest prayers, desires, thoughts or hopes" (Eph. 3:20, TLB).

Some months ago a young couple in our church were facing what was to them some imposing financial obligations. They had just moved to our community and had incurred the normal moving expenses; they were expecting their second child in a few weeks with the accompanying medical bills and on top of this, the IRS informed them that they owed several hundred dollars in additional taxes, due immediately.

It was almost more than they could handle. They came to me in real concern, without any idea how to secure the needed funds. We prayed about it together and in a few days they received a seven-hundred-dollar refund check from the IRS

[3]William A. Ogden, "He Is Able to Deliver Thee," in "Hymns of Glorious Praise," (Gospel Publishing House, Springfield, Mo., 1969), p. 182.

with a letter of apology and explanation.

The check was enough to cover their unpaid moving expenses and the cost of the baby with some left over. Truly, God is sufficient if we will but ask!

GOD'S PATIENCE

Some may ask, "If God is good, and willing, and sufficient, why, then, doesn't prayer work for me? Why aren't my prayers answered?"

The Bible teaches that God answers prayer in response to our needs: ". . . he will rise and give him whatever he needs" (Luke 11:8). Often the things we pray for are not needs, but selfish whims, outgrowths of our gluttonous life style. James writes, "You ask and do not receive, because you ask wrongly, to spend it on your passions" (James 4:3). Then again what you interpret as no answer may simply be a delayed answer. Luke 18:7 teaches that God will answer prayer ". . . though he bear long with [us]" (KJV). There are undoubtedly several reasons God delays His answers, some of which are:

To weed out our trite and insincere petitions. Both the parables in Luke 11 and in Luke 18 suggest that God will not hear or answer that which we do not care enough to pray about conscientiously and persistently. If our requests are not important enough to be prayed about more than once, if we can't remember them from one prayer time to the next, then they probably aren't important enough to merit an answer.

Perhaps another reason is to teach us the proper attitude in prayer. In church, we sometimes sing an old chorus which goes:

"Have thine own way, Lord,
Have thine own way.
Thou art the potter

I am the clay.
Mold me and make me
after thy will.
While I am waiting
Yielded and still.[4]"

In our worship tradition we have many such choruses committed to memory and we sing them without the aid of printed music or lyrics, consequently individual worshipers sometimes misunderstand the lyrics and learn them wrong. One young boy, of ten or eleven, was overhead singing,

"Thou art the porter. . . ."

This all too often portrays our attitude in prayer. We act as if God is some kind of divine busboy whose only reason for existence is to serve our whims, as if He were some kind of genie constantly at our disposal. God resists this kind of prayer, delays His answers until we have learned that we cannot manipulate Him; until we have prayed ourselves into exhausted surrender, finally saying, ". . . nevertheless, not what I will, but what thou wilt" (Mark 14:36 KJV).

A third possible reason is so He can supply all of our needs, not just the ones we are consciously praying about. He wants to give us "bread" but not just bread. His ministry to us is limited to our availability and many of us spend time with God only when we are pressed by urgent needs. Knowing this, He delays His "answers" until He has had time to make Himself known, until we have spent time enough in His presence to develop further our fragile faith.

Prayer does not exist to meet our needs, rather our needs serve to call us to prayer. Prayer will provide God with the opportunity to supply our needs, but that is not so much the purpose of prayer as it is a natural consequence of it. The highest purpose of prayer is intimacy with God and our urgent needs call us to Him and keep us in His presence until, ". . . [we] know that [He is] God. . ." (Ps. 46:10).

GOD'S PROVISION

By suggesting that God's "answers" are the consequence of prayer rather than its goal or purpose; we do not mean to belittle their significance or God's faithful generosity. He will answer our prayer for "daily bread."

Notice how careful Jesus is to indicate the amount of provision: ". . . he will rise and give him whatever he needs" (Luke 11:8). Not less than we need, lest He undermine our trust, but not more either, lest we feel self-sufficient.

Most of us are uncomfortable with that kind of provision. We want a little extra, something to put away so we will not be caught empty-handed and embarrassed the next time life makes its unannounced demands. But God gives us only "daily bread," only enough for the present situation. He will not give us extra, lest we make His "extra" our security and not Him.

Life for many of us is not abundant, His promised grace apparently insufficient, our emotional bank accounts constantly overdrawn. Why? Hasn't He promised to supply all of our needs?

He has, and He will, but His promised provisions are relational; that is to say, we experience them only as a consequence, an outgrowth of our relationship to Him. The Psalmist wrote, "The Lord is my shepherd; I shall not want" (Ps. 23:1 KJV). Not being in want was a direct result of David's right relationship with the Lord! God's provisions are not so much a gift apart from himself as they are an expression of himself.

And He only makes His provision sufficient for the present, one day at a time. ". . . and as thy days, so shall thy strength

39

be'' (Deut. 33:25 KJV). If you are overcome with cares, and if you feel incapable of coping with life, perhaps it is because you are still trying to carry the past. Learn to live one day at a time! The past can't be changed, only forgiven. If you've never asked God's forgiveness for your past, do so right now. If you have asked, then accept it. By an act of your will stop living in the past, stop punishing yourself.

Others may find life unbearable, not because of the past, but because of the fear of the future. Frightful projections and fearful imaginings about what might happen are not only foolish, but are often emotionally and spiritually destructive. God's only way of helping you cope with things that have not yet happened and which probably won't happen is to direct you to ''. . . take every thought captive. . .'' (2 Cor. 10:5). Live in the present. Find God sufficient for today and trust Him to be sufficient for tomorrow when it comes.

> "What have I to dread,
> what have I to fear,
> Leaning on the everlasting arms,
> I have blessed peace
> with my Lord so near,
> Leaning on the everlasting arms."[5]

Jesus concludes this parable by saying, "If you then, who are evil, know how to give good gifts to your children, how much more will the heavenly Father give the Holy Spirit to those who ask him!" (Luke 11:13). Matthew recorded Christ's words this way: ''. . . how much more will your Father who is in heaven give good things to those who ask him!'' (7:11).

---

[5]Elisha A. Hoffman, Anthony J. Showalter, "Leaning on The Everlasting Arms," in "Hymns of Glorious Praise," (Gospel Publishing House, Springfield, Missouri, 1969), p. 298.

The God Who Forgives

"Therefore this kingdom of heaven may be compared to a king who wished to settle accounts with his servants. When he began the reckoning, one was brought to him who owed him ten thousand talents; and as he could not pay, his lord ordered him to be sold, with his wife and children and all that he had, and payment to be made. So the servant fell on his knees, imploring him, 'Lord, have patience with me, and I will pay you everything.' And out of pity for him the lord of that servant released him and forgave him the debt. But that same servant, as he went out, came upon one of his fellow servants who owed him a hundred denarii; and seizing him by the throat he said, 'Pay what you owe.' So his fellow servant fell down and besought him, 'Have patience with me and I will pay you.' He refused and went and put him in prison till he should pay the debt. When his fellow servants saw what had taken place, they were greatly distressed, and they went and reported to their lord all that had taken place. Then his lord summoned him and said to him, 'You wicked servant! I forgave you all that debt because you besought me; and should not you have had mercy on your fellow servant, as I had mercy on you?' And in anger his lord delivered him to the jailers, till he should pay all his debt. So also my heavenly Father will do to every one of you, if you do not forgive your brother from your heart.''

—Matt. 18:23-35

T HIS is one of the most incredible stories I have ever read, so incredible, in fact, that if it weren't in the Bible I wouldn't believe it.

It's not surprising that this king became suspicious and asked for an audit. The amazing thing is that the servant escaped detection for so long. He had embezzled "ten thousand talents" (Matt. 18:24).

A talent of gold, according to Bible scholar Finis Dake, was worth $29,850, making ten thousand talents equal to $298,500,000.[1] David A. Redding gives a much more conservative figure, in the neighborhood of two million dollars, still a staggering sum in light of the fact that the "total annual taxes of Judea, Idumea, Samaria, Galilee, and Perea, all together, amounted to only 800 talents."[2] According to footnotes in the Revised Standard Version, "[a] talent was more than fifteen years' wages of a laborer."[3] Whatever figures we accept, the sum is overwhelming, even in our age of inflation.

The only thing more overwhelming is the king's mercy. He has a great heart, and like God, ". . . is longsuffering to us-ward, not willing that any should perish, but that all should come to repentance" (2 Pet. 3:9 KJV). When this servant pleaded with him, from bended knee, he was moved with pity and ". . . released him and forgave him the debt" (Matt. 18:27).

[1]Finis Jennings Dake, "Dake's Annotated Reference Bible," (Dake Bible Sales, Inc., Atlanta, Georgia, 1963), p. 20, column 4 in The New Testament.
[2]David A. Redding, "The Parables He Told," (Fleming H. Revell Co., Westwood, New Jersey, n.d.), p. 49.
[3]Department of Christian Education of the National Council of Churches of Christ in the United States of America, "Revised Standard Version of The New Testament," (Thomas Nelson and Sons, Toronto, New York, Edinburgh, 1971).

Now the story takes its most incredible turn. The forgiven servant leaves the king's presence, not overwhelmed by the king's act of mercy, but smug, feeling that it was his own resourcefulness which got him off.

As he was leaving the court he caught sight of a man who owed him "a hundred denarii" (about $17.00 according to Dake).[4] Mere pocket change in comparison to his own insurmountable debt, yet he grabs the poor fellow by the throat and demands immediate payment! The frightened debtor pleads for patience, promising to pay. Not a chance! The recently forgiven servant has him thrown into debtors' prison.

His merciless act did not go unobserved and those who saw it were horrified. As soon as they recovered their speech they made it known to the king who ordered the servant brought before him and in anger, which surpassed in intensity even his mercy, he roared, "You wicked servant! I forgave you all that debt because you besought me; and should not you have had mercy on your fellow servant, as I had on you?" (Matt. 18:32, 33). Then the king delivered him to the jailers till he should pay all his debt.

Jesus then concludes this unusual story with some of the most terrifying words in the whole Bible, "So also my heavenly Father will do to every one of you, if you do not forgive your brother from your heart" (Matt. 18:35).

Here, and in several other places (e.g., in The Lord's Prayer and in the Sermon on the Mount) the Lord makes our forgiveness of others mandatory. Let us consider why.

BECAUSE GOD HAS FORGIVEN US

It is impossible to appreciate God's grace and forgiveness until we understand the awful significance of our sin. As

[4]Dake, "Dake's Annotated Reference Bible," p. 20.

preposterous as it may seem, we all have a $298,500,000 sin debt! "For whoever keeps the whole law but fails in one point has become guilty of all of it" (James 2:10). In God's sight we are as criminal as this evil servant whom we find so detestable. Only when we comprehend this, painful though it is, can we grasp something of the greatness of His forgiveness.

Sometimes it seems we take His forgiveness for granted. Such an attitude is fine when it is a product of our faith in the greatness of His grace, for as David wrote, ". . . [the] Lord [is] good and ready to forgive; and plenteous in mercy . . ." (Ps. 86:5 KJV).

Unfortunately, much of our faith is based on our own sense of merit. Our sins are always inconsequential in comparison to others, or there were mitigating circumstances, or we were victimized. "Of course God will forgive us, how could he do anything else under the circumstances?" Such an attitude makes a mockery of sin; it reduces God to a mere figurehead.

Whenever you are tempted to treat sin lightly look back to Golgotha. If you are ever tempted to think God treats sin casually, remember Christ on the cross. That's God's attitude toward sin! It must be judged and punished! "Go ahead, drive the nails, erect the cross, hang Him up there against the backdrop of history for all men to see." The "Word made flesh" becomes God's final word about sin, a broken bleeding word, a dying word screaming out a final warning!

And it becomes God's finest word about love, "Greater love has no man than this, that a man lay down his life for his friends" (John 15:13). "But God shows his love for us in that while we were yet sinners Christ died for us" (Rom. 5:8). "God so loved the world that he gave his only Son . . ." (John 3:16).

God could not be just and allow sin to go unpunished, "For the wages [consequences] of sin is death . . ." (Rom. 6:23);

yet neither could He be loving and allow all mankind to die in their sins, without any chance of salvation.

Only the great heart of God could find a solution which satisfied both His justice and His love. Only the willingness of Jesus could make that hypothetical solution a reality. Christ on the cross became the ultimate reality expressing both God's justice and His love. He met God's justice by suffering the full penalty for our sins and He expressed God's love by becoming the "way" of our salvation.

Such forgiveness radically affects the recipient's whole life. It deals a fatal wound to self-sufficiency and fleshly pride. It affects how he sees himself, God and his neighbor. He who is truly a recipient of grace will also become its instrument, forgiving others, not in an effort to be forgiven, but because he is forgiven.

The problem in this parable is not with the king's forgiveness, ". . . the lord of that servant released him and forgave him the debt" (Matt. 18:27), but with the servant. He mistook the king's mercy for weakness. He confused his own clever resourcefulness with the king's grace and ended up destroying himself. Such a man is soon found out. He cannot hide his attitude, it reveals itself in the way he treats others.

Likewise he who truly accepts the forgiveness of God will ". . . be kind . . . tenderhearted, forgiving . . ." (Eph. 4:32).

God's forgiveness is a historical fact, it was finished on the cross. The only prerequisite is faith to appropriate it. We need do nothing but accept it, and once accepted it becomes a way of life, ". . . forgiving each other as the Lord has forgiven [us] . . ." (Col. 3:13).

TO FACILITATE CHANGE

Many of us have mistakenly believed that repentance precedes forgiveness when in fact the exact opposite is true. Forgiveness provides the motivation and power which makes repentance a reality. God forgives us, not because we have changed, but so we can!

One of the key terms in this parable is "loosed"; the Revised Standard Version says "released" (verse 27). Once exposed, the servant made a passionate plea, promising to repay everything. The king had pity on him and ". . . released him and forgave him the debt" (Matt. 18:27) because he knew repayment was impossible. A schedule of payments would in reality be nothing more than a life sentence under conditions which would make further criminal activity almost inevitable.

I recently saw a cartoon which depicted an attorney pleading his client's case. Apparently this was at least a second offense because the attorney was saying, "The only reason the defendant knocked off that filling station was because Your Honor ordered him to make restitution to his first victim."

Often the real reason people continue in the same destructive patterns of behavior is because we force them to focus on their past. When we fail to forgive we imprison them, we sentence them to a lifetime of repeated failures. The past is like a role they are forced to play again and again. The only way to rewrite the script, to "loose" them, is to forgive and accept them as they are. Once recast in the role of the forgiven rather than the condemned, they have a chance to live productive and creative lives.

Life's rewrites are often a joint effort between God and men. John gives a beautiful example of this in the eleventh chapter of his Gospel. Jesus is standing outside of the tomb of His friend Lazarus, who has now been dead four days. After praying He lifts His voice and cries loudly, ". . . Lazarus, come out"

(John 11:43). In the graphic words of John, "The dead man came out, his hands and feet bound with bandages, and his face wrapped with a cloth . . ." (John 11:44). Then Jesus turned His attention to the family and friends in attendance. "Unbind him, and let him go" (John 11:44).

The raising of Lazarus is a symbol of salvation, the new birth. As only Jesus could raise Lazarus from the dead, so only God can raise a man from the tomb of His transgressions, only He can give new life and call men forth from the deadness of their sins. Yet the raising of Lazarus also involved people other than Jesus. Prior to the miracle, Christ drafted some of the crowd to roll the stone away and immediately following Lazarus' appearance He commanded others to "unbind him." Lazarus' return to life was not complete until his family and friends freed him.

Many are incapable of fully experiencing salvation until someone "looses" them. Often they spend years bound in the bandages of the past, after God has given them new life, because unforgiving people will not let them go.

Christ calls us to "loose" them from the grave clothes of sin, to unbind them from the imprisoning failures of the past. Forgiveness is our most effective instrument, for when we forgive we free them, we rip off the chains of the past and allow them to start fresh.

Realism forces me to admit that even full forgiveness did not change this wicked servant. The entire parable is a dismaying account of his continued evil. He is not an isolated individual either. Life is filled with those who seem immune even to the miracle of forgiveness.

This, however, must not discourage us nor lead us to try other less scriptural strategies. Fear, judgment and punishment are not only unscriptural but ineffective. Forgiveness will fail, some men are determined to sin even against love, but when they do, neither time nor eternity has any resources left. "For if we sin deliberately after receiving the knowledge of the truth, there no longer remains a sacrifice for sins" (Heb. 10:26). That is to say, if the forgiveness of God as expressed in the crucified Christ cannot invoke in us a response of surrender and commitment, then nothing can. God has no resources left; Christ was His ultimate effort.

All that remains is ". . . a fearful prospect of judgment, and a fury of fire which will consume the adversaries" (Heb. 10:27). This does not occur as a corrective, rehabilitative measure but as the inevitable and eternal consequence of deliberate sin. The king delivered that wicked servant ". . . to the torturers till he should pay all his debt" (Matt. 18:34, Jerusalem Bible).

TO FREE US FROM THE PAST

The thrust of forgiveness is designed not only to free the one forgiven, but to liberate the forgiver as well. Christ knows we cannot experience the abundant life as long as our lives are filled to the brim with bitterness. Anger and vindictiveness leave no room for joy and love. Hands clenched, ready to take revenge, can never reach out and receive the blessings of life.

If, as we've already concluded, judgment imprisons the unforgiven, then it must be equally true that the accuser becomes the jailer. In reality, are not both the accused and the accuser prisoners of the past, living out their lives in the narrow, suffocating confines of yesterday's wrongs? The accuser holds the key, not only to the cell of the accused, but to his own as well. If and when he forgives, the door to life and freedom will open to him as well as to the accused. Once he releases his grudge he is no longer obligated to be the jailer; he is free to get on with the business of living!

Many marriages fit into this warden/prisoner pattern. Wrongs, real or imagined, are carefully kept and embellished through the years, until the relationship is hardly more than a prison of pain. Unforgiven acts are built into higher and higher walls which imprison both parties in roles they are bitter and unhappy with. Often such neurotic marriages end in divorce but very little is really accomplished if forgiveness is not part of the settlement. If it is not, old wounds and the accompanying behavioral patterns are taken into any new relationship, threatening it almost from the beginning.

It must be conceded, though, that some people are apparently able to carry grudges and still live relatively successful lives. In fact, deep-seated anger or hatred has served, in some cases, as motivation. Yet, I cannot help but wonder at the quality of their lives. Do they know anything of the joys of close human associations, do they like themselves, do they have a sense of fulfillment or peace? I think not!

Some time ago, a lady came for counseling. Though blessed with many of the finer things of life she was nonetheless very unhappy. She spent almost the entire hour recounting, in deadly detail, every slight she had suffered in the past fifteen or twenty years. When, near the end of the session, I gently suggested that forgiveness might be the key to finding happiness, she hastened to assure me that she was a Christian and had already forgiven everyone who had ever wronged her. Obviously, this lady either had a very distorted concept of forgiveness or else she was very dishonest with herself—perhaps both. If she had truly forgiven them there would not have been such intensity in her accounts of the incidents; in fact she probably would not have found it necessary to share them at all.

If you catch yourself repeatedly reliving the past, especially those incidents where you were wronged, then let me suggest that you need to forgive as freely and fully as God has forgiven you. Forgiveness means to let go, to let go of the hurts, the grudges, the feelings, even the memories. As long as you are reliving the hurtful incidents, either in memory or conversation, you haven't released them or truly forgiven the one who caused them.

THE LIBERATING ACT OF FORGIVENESS

Many seem to have the mistaken concept that forgiveness is a feeling; it is not, it is an act of the will. Corrie ten Boom includes in *The Hiding Place* just such an incident:

It was at a church in Munich that I saw him, the former S.S. man who had stood guard at the shower room door in the processing center at Ravensbruck. He was the first of our actual jailers that I had seen since that time. And suddenly it was all there—the roomful of mocking men, the heaps of clothing, Betsie's pain-blanched face.

He came up to me as the church was emptying, beaming and bowing. "How grateful I am for your message, Fraulein," he said. "To think that, as you say, He has washed my sins away!"

His hand was thrust out to shake mine. And I, who had preached so often to the people in Bloemindaal the need to forgive, kept my hand at my side.

Even as the angry vengeful thoughts boiled through me, I saw the sin of them. Jesus Christ had died for this man; was I going to ask for more? Lord Jesus, I prayed, forgive me and help me to forgive him.

I tried to smile, I struggled to raise my hand. I could not. I felt nothing, not the slightest spark of warmth or charity.

And so again I breathed a silent prayer. Jesus, I cannot forgive him. Give me Your forgiveness.

As I took his hand the most incredible thing happened. From my shoulder along my arm and through my hand a current seemed to pass from me to him, while into my heart sprang a love for this stranger that almost overwhelmed me.[5]

The feelings of forgiveness almost never precede the actual act. We must, by an act of our will, pronounce forgiveness and only after that can we expect the proper emotional accompaniment. If you wait for the supposed emotional motivation you will quite probably spend much of your life in a self-made prison. Learn to act out your forgiveness and you will discover a life of joy and freedom.

The inability to forgive is one of the major sources of unhappiness and inner turmoil and as such, it is frequently the focal point of my counseling. I often share these very simple steps which I have found to facilitate forgiveness:

First, honestly confess your feelings. Many people, especially Christians, realize that feelings of bitterness and resentment are not Christ-like and so they deny and repress them. Of course, there can be no act of forgiveness until such feelings are acknowledged and the need to forgive faced up to.

By confession I do not mean a mere recital of hurts as much as I mean a reliving of them, emotionally and vocally in the presence of God. Tell God specifically what happened and how it made you feel, then and now. This usually takes some time and is emotionally draining, but it is very important if we are to get our feelings out in the open, before God, where He can deal with them.

Secondly, acknowledge that you are powerless to change

[5]Corrie ten Boom, "The Hiding Place," (Washington Depot, Conn: Chosen Books, 1971), p. 215.

what you feel. Usually a person does not seek counseling until he has exhausted every other resource and so his very presence is a nonverbal confession of his inability to deal creatively with his feelings. The next step, then, is to tell God and give Him permission to change how you feel.

Some people have real difficulty at this point because they are afraid if they do not punish the offending party no one will. They are truly afraid to give God permission to change their feelings because they fear He will and they are not yet ready to release the object of their judgment. Giving God permission to change us must be an act of our will, just as pronouncing forgiveness is.

Thirdly, forgive each injury specifically in prayer to God. For example: "God, I forgive him for humiliating me. God, I forgive him for lying about me. God, I forgive . . . ." Continue in this way until every remembered offense has been dealt with.

People often ask if they should tell the other persons involved that they have forgiven them. A pretty good rule of thumb is: if the other person or persons are aware of your bitter feelings then by all means tell them. But if you have kept your hurt secret, don't tell. An act of forgiveness toward an individual who is unaware of hurting or offending you sounds more like a gesture of judgment than one of love.

Many times in counseling, after utilizing these three steps, I have witnessed personal transformations which can only be called miraculous. The persons involved have entered my office disillusioned and bitter, weighted down with grudges, some which they've carried for years. An hour later they were free from anger and alive to life and God.

I am not suggesting that this is an instantaneous, once-and-for-all cure-all, but I am offering it as a strategy for handling vindictiveness and as a workable way of practicing forgiveness. These steps (which are really a form of prayer), like prayer, open us to the resources of God. They give Him a chance to express His forgiveness through us, bringing abundant life to all concerned.

The Vulnerable God

And when it was evening he came with the twelve. And as they were at table eating, Jesus said, "Truly, I say to you, one of you will betray me, one who is eating with me." They began to be sorrowful, and to say to him one after another, "Is it I?" He said to them, "It is one of the twelve, one who is dipping bread into the dish with me. For the Son of man goes as it is written of him, but woe to that man by whom the Son of man is betrayed! It would have been better for that man if he had not been born." And as they were eating, he took bread, and blessed, and broke it, and gave it to them, and said, "Take; this is my body." And he took a cup, and when he had given thanks he gave it to them, and they all drank of it. And he said to them, "This is my blood of the covenant which is poured out for many. Truly, I say to you, I shall not drink again of the fruit of the vine until that day when I drink it new in the kingdom of God." And when they had sung a hymn, they went out to the Mount of Olives.

—Mark 14:17-26

HOLY communion, without question, is one of the most meaningful acts of Christian worship. It's symbolic language speaks volumes; about God, Christ, salvation, and about ourselves.

John 3:16 says that ". . . God so loved the world that he gave his only Son. . . ." Eloquent, but less so than the simplest communion service, for there the love of God is given and received afresh. Each time the bread is broken and shared we remember His love gift; each time it's received we experience, by faith, the coming of Christ anew. In some mysterious way it reminds us that Christ was both the giver and the gift. ". . . He [Christ] took bread, and blessed, and broke it, and gave it to them and said, 'Take, this is my body.' And he took a cup and . . . gave it to them. . . . And he said to them, 'This is my blood of the covenant, which is poured out for many' " (Mark 14:22-24). "No one takes it [my life] from me, but I lay it down of my own accord. . ." (John 10:18).

Every time we celebrate communion we are remembering Christ. We remember the preincarnate Christ; we remember the glory He had with the Father before creation (John 17:5). We remember the "Word made flesh," the Christ who lived as we live, experiencing all the uncertainties of life, all the temptation men are subject to. We remember the crucified Christ, He who became sin so we could become the righteousness of God in Him (see 2 Cor. 5:21). We remember the resurrected Christ, seen of John, "When I saw him, I fell at his feet as though dead. But he laid his right hand upon me, saying, 'Fear not, I am the first and the last, and the living one; I died and behold I am alive for evermore, and I have the keys of Death and Hades" (Rev. 1:17, 18). We remember the ascended, exalted Christ, ". . . God has highly exalted him and bestowed on him the name which is above every name" (Phil. 2:9). We remember His promise to come again, ". . . I will come again and will take you to myself, that where I am you may be also" (John 14:3).

Communion tells us that sin is serious, demanding radical measures if its deadly consequences are to be cured. "Christ redeemed us from the curse . . . having become a curse for us—for it is written, 'Cursed be every one who hangs on a tree' " (Gal. 3:13). It makes us aware of our sinfulness, but it also reminds us of our capacity for intimacy and fellowship with God. "He who eats my flesh and drinks my blood abides in me, and I in him" (John 6:56).

And this is just the beginning—the smallest trickle in a truly surging stream of truth. The communion is inexhaustible, a source of never-ending inspiration. It is a most obvious symbol of God's vulnerability. Consider if you will:

THE VULNERABLE CHRIST

". . . The Word," according to John, "became flesh and dwelt among us. . ." (John 1:14). The unseen, unapproachable, invincible God drew near, came within reach. And we "handled" him, misused him, abused him, broke him, and finally killed him. We hung Him up on a cross and left Him there to die!

Christ's vulnerability is obvious. Who is more defenseless,

more helpless than a tiny baby, especially one forced by circumstances to be born in a barn? Is anyone more susceptible to others than one who, like Jesus, is dependent on others for even the simplest necessities of life? Without the boy's small lunch the multitude would not have been fed, without Simon's boat Christ would have been smothered by the crowd and unable to teach, without a borrowed ass there would have been no triumphal entry and no Palm Sunday, without a borrowed room there would have been no Last Supper and no communion. Truly Jesus was dependent upon the ministry of others, ". . . Foxes have holes, and birds of the air have nests; but the Son of man has nowhere to lay his head" (Matt. 8:20).

No one is more vulnerable than the person who cares, who opens his heart to the world around him. We all know people who have stopped caring and not because they are hard or bitter, but out of self-defense—they don't want to be hurt any more. But to stop caring is to stop living. He who cannot cry cannot truly laugh and he who neither laughs nor cries is not alive.

Jesus was the most alive person this world has ever known, and much of the reason was His capacity to laugh and cry. As paradoxical as it sounds, Jesus was probably both the happiest and saddest man the world has ever known. Isaiah calls Him "a man of sorrows" and Jesus speaks of Himself saying, "My joy is full." Sorrow does not cancel out joy nor vice versa, rather each enlarges the individual's capacity for the other. Christ cared deeply and as a consequence, He was very susceptible to those around Him. He rejoiced with those who rejoiced, and He wept with those who wept.

When Lazarus died Jesus shared Mary and Martha's burden of grief. "When Jesus saw her weeping, and the Jews who came with her also weeping he was deeply moved in spirit and troubled and he said, 'Where have you laid him?' They said to him, 'Lord, come and see.' Jesus wept'' (John 11:33-35).

"Jesus wept."

What more is there to say about our Lord's emotional vulnerability?

It goes without saying that the consequences of Christ's vulnerability reached their maximum during His sufferings just before and during His crucifixion. He was betrayed by a friend, denied by a disciple, forsaken by His followers, rejected by His nation, tried and condemned by Judaism and finally executed by Rome. He suffered in every way imaginable—emotionally, psychologically, physically and spiritually!

Yet the cross was not an accident. Christ was not a helpless victim but a willing sacrifice. ". . . I lay down my life. . . . No man taketh it from me, but I lay it down of myself'' (John 10:17, 18 KJV). Golgotha was a place of death, violent, dark death, but it was not a disaster; it was divine provision!

THE VULNERABLE FATHER

God is not so obviously vulnerable, but remember, parents often suffer more for their children than they do for themselves. Generally a parent can be injured most deeply through his children. Let his children suffer defeat or disappointment, and his anguish is greater than theirs. If his children are attacked or maligned his hurt is often deeper than theirs. With this in mind, who can doubt the Father's vulnerability?

My comprehension of God's sufferings is best when I relive the Old Testament story of Abraham and Isaac. God commanded Abraham to go to the mountains of Moriah and there to offer his son Isaac for a burnt offering. After three days' journey they arrive at the designated mountain and leaving the servants, Abraham and Isaac began the long climb toward the place of worship.

As they climb Isaac turns to Abraham and asks, "Behold, the fire and the wood; but where is the lamb for a burnt offering?" (Gen. 22:7). ". . . My son," Abraham answers, "God will provide himself a lamb. . ." (Gen. 22:8).

Was Abraham's response honest? I wonder if he really believed God would provide, or if this was the irrational wishing of a desperate man?

The long climb is finally completed and construction on the altar begun. It was undoubtedly the most carefully constructed altar of all time. Abraham built deliberately, delayed as long as possible, still it was finally finished, the wood carefully laid, the fire ready.

The Scriptures do not tell us what happened then. Did Isaac ask again about the lamb? Did he, by this time, have some awful premonition?

What did Abraham do? Did he face Isaac, look him in the eye, place his hands on those broad young shoulders? Did unbidden tears course down his dusty cheeks and lose themselves in his beard? Did he embrace Isaac, caress him, express his love? Did he try to explain, try to make him understand?

We have no way of knowing; the Scriptures do not tell us how Abraham got Isaac on the altar. They are silent, because silence expresses the awful emotional impact more eloquently than any narrative.

In my mind I can see it clearly: Isaac on the altar, bound, as still as death; Abraham—weeping, the upraised hand, holding the dagger, trembling, delaying the deadly descent one eternal second longer—

"Abraham . . . lay not thy hand upon the lad, neither do thou anything unto him. . . . And Abraham lifted up his eyes, and looked, and behold behind him a ram caught in a thicket by his horns: and Abraham went and took the ram, and offered him up for a burnt offering in the stead of his son" (Gen. 22:11-13).

Did God experience something like this as He journeyed with Jesus to Golgotha? What did He feel when hard Roman hands flung His Son down, when the spike was positioned and the heavy hammer raised? Did He search eternity for a God greater than He, one who would call Him by name and rescue Him from this awful dilemma? There was only silence, finally broken by the sound of a solitary hammer striking a nail.

Then there was bedlam, the tormented attacks of those crucified with Jesus, the gambling of the soldiers, the verbal viciousness of the taunting mobs and the intercessory prayers of the crucified one. God couldn't stand it, couldn't bear to look at the broken, bleeding body of His Son, so He draped this planet in mourning. ". . . and there was a darkness over all the earth until the ninth hour" (Luke 23:44 KJV).

"And at the ninth hour Jesus cried with a loud voice, 'Eloi, Eloi, lama sabachthani?' which means, 'My God, my God, why hast thou forsaken me?' " (Mark 15:34).

How did our heavy-hearted God feel then, at the ninth hour? What conflicting emotions raged in His heart and mind? How He must have longed to tear the darkness away, to gently lift the trembling body of Jesus from the cross, to heal His wounds, to show He had not forsaken Him.

But He didn't! Christ's poignant plea went unanswered, the darkness remained. What love God must have for our lost race to endure such pain and suffering to bring us salvation!

Jean-Baptiste Calmence, the hero of Albert Camus' book, *The Fall*, says, "Do you know that in my little village, during a punitive operation, a German officer courteously asked an old woman to please choose which of her two sons would be shot as a hostage? Choose!—Can you imagine that? that one? No, this one!''[1]

Can you see her in the travail of such a decision? How does she choose? The first born—but no! She remembers the midwife placing him in her arms, her husband's proud and thankful eyes, her own feelings of fulfillment. Her second son? No, for he was always the thoughtful one. Bouncing in from school with a fist full of wild flowers and a shy smile. Her oldest son—her youngest son? How can she choose? Such an offer is not courteous, but sadistic!

Such is the position God found Himself in that Friday. Christ or the world? He could not save them both. One or the other would die.

A NEW STRATEGY

I remember and relive all of this each time I approach communion. I wonder, "Must Jesus bear the cross alone, and all the world go free?"[2] Does this not say something to us about our responsibilities, our way of relating to others? Isn't the "agape" love supposed to be our style? Isn't Christ our model? "For I have given you an example, that you also should do as I have done to you" (John 13:15).

Some time ago we were celebrating the communion in our Sunday evening service. In preparation for partaking I reminded the worshipers that the broken bread and wine were symbols of our Lord's vulnerability and as such they called us to relate to one another and the world from a similar stance of loving openness.

I shared how such a style had enhanced my ministry in the first church I served. My inexperience and youth, combined with the pettiness of the congregation, had produced a crisis. At a special communion service I apologized for my failures and asked forgiveness. My sincerity and humility (I truly felt like a

[1]Albert Camus, "The Fall," translated by Justin O'Brien (The Modern Library—Random House, New York, 1956), p. 11.
[2]Thomas Shepherd and George W. Allen, "Must Jesus Bear the Cross Alone?" in "Hymns of Glorious Praise" (Gospel Publishing House, Springfield, Missouri, 1969), p. 352.

failure) disarmed them, took the fuse out of the time bomb of their anger. They forgave me and began confessing their own failures. Fellowship was restored and the next two years were a time of truly meaningful ministry. We were not without problems but that vulnerable style enabled us to deal with them creatively.

Now, as the first steps in living out our vulnerability, I asked the worshipers to take a piece of bread and go to another person and risk sharing something intimate. It could be a deep need for which they desired prayer, it could be a confession, it could be the sharing of something really significant, anything which required them to trust the other person.

Slowly, one by one, they made their way to the communion table for bread and then to one another. There were tears, and laughter, embraces and prayer. There was intimacy—that quality of relating which nourishes the soul. We broke bread and fellowshiped in the truest biblical sense, and it was possible because we followed the divine model and became vulnerable to one another.

Don't be misled, all efforts at relating to others on this level are not rewarded with such intimate fellowship. Christ was crucified and all who follow him will experience rejection. Yet there is no other way to experience a truly biblical fellowship and no other way to have a spiritual ministry. It was God's style and must become ours!

The Good Shepherd

What man of you, having a hundred sheep, if he has lost one of them, does not leave the ninety-nine in the wilderness, and go after the one which is lost, until he finds it? And when he has found it, he lays it on his shoulders, rejoicing. And when he comes home, he calls together his friends and his neighbors, saying to them, "Rejoice with me, for I have found my sheep which was lost." Just so, I tell you, there will be more joy in heaven over one sinner who repents than over ninety-nine righteous persons who need no repentance.

—Luke 15:4-7

JESUS was a thorny problem for the religious crowd of His day. They couldn't make up their minds about Him, He was a paradox. He reinterpreted the laws of the Sabbath, expounded the Scriptures in discomforting ways, forgave sins and fellowshiped openly with known sinners. He claimed oneness with God and forgave sins, which made him a blasphemer in their eyes. Yet, He performed miracles and healings which traditionally authenticated a man's ministry.

Some of the Pharisees said, "This man is not from God, for he does not keep the sabbath." But others said, "How can a man who is a sinner do such signs?" There was a division among them. (John 9:16)

Such a controversy prompted Jesus to share the insightful parables of Luke 15, including this one concerning the lost sheep. The sinners and outcasts were drawn to Him by His compassionate words of hope, and His acceptance of them confused and angered the Pharisees and scribes who complained, ". . . This man receives sinners and eats with them" (Luke 15:2).

Jesus employed these parables in hopes of gaining the

understanding and support of the disapproving religious leaders. They missed His point but these stories have remained and serve today to help the church understand her Lord and His mission. They give dimension and definition to our relationship with Him and the lost.

THE LOST

It seems religious people have a tendency to look down on the unchurched. This is not always true but it is common enough to call us to re-examine our attitudes in light of Jesus' attitude. He is the believer's example and we need to align our attitudes with His.

Jesus loved the lost, not in a condescending manner, but with a love which valued them as persons of worth and potential. To Him, they seemed more weak than wicked, more empty than evil. Sin was the hated enemy, not the sinner. The sinner was the victim, lost and hurting, in need of love and salvation.

Matthew writes, "When he saw the crowds, he had compassion for them, because they were harassed and helpless, like sheep without a shepherd" (9:36). The Living Bible says, "And what pity he felt for the crowds that came, because their problems were so great and they didn't know what to do or where to go for help. They were like sheep without a shepherd."

The only real anger Christ ever expressed was toward the self-righteous who denied their sin, who pretended to be something they were not. With the tax collectors and prostitutes He was compassionate and forgiving.

Just this week I returned from a church convention in Oklahoma City. The convention center, one of the first evidences of renovation, towered modern and gleaming amid the squalor and decay of the inner city. My motel was four blocks from the center and each day as I walked that distance I was confronted with the painful reality of life without God.

The streets and sidewalks were littered with broken glass and other debris. Whole blocks were empty, overgrown with weeds, huge holes revealed where buildings once had stood, signs from which the paint was peeling promised new buildings sometime in the future. And the inhabitants, the street people, were as worn as the neighborhood.

Unkempt drunks and derelicts lounged in the alleys and doorways, others slept on the sidewalks. Prostitutes, looking desperate and tired, hustled business blatantly. One stepped smartly out of a trashy bar onto the dirty sidewalk. A glance was enough to see it was just an act, that beneath the heavy makeup she was hurting. She couldn't have been older than thirty but she had aged terribly and when she smiled I turned away in revulsion, for she had only an ugly gaping hole where her teeth should have been.

I struggled wtih my feelings of contempt, finally confessing and asking forgiveness. These were the kind of people Jesus died for, the kind of people He had compassion on and I could feel nothing in my heart but loathing and disgust. I went to Him, stayed in His presence until I could see those poor misfits as He saw them, not as drunken bums and cheap whores, but ". . . like sheep without a shepherd."

Of course a person need not reach such obvious depths to be lost. In fact, many apparently rich and successful people experience a lostness unimagined by those who inhabit skid row. The outcasts still have the illusion, however faint, that if they could make something of themselves, get a job, a home, a family, then life would be meaningful. The super-rich, the successful, the sophisticated know better and their lostness is sharper and more bitter because of it. They have no more worlds to conquer, they have achieved all their goals and still their lostness remains, and even expands. It's no wonder such people take their own lives. They have gained the whole world and not found inner satisfaction. Life holds no hope for them.

A pastor received a phone call from a woman who was in a state of obvious emotional distress. When he arrived at the address she had given him he found himself in an elite neighborhood in front of a beautiful home. The door was opened by a butler who showed him into the library and told him the Mrs. would be with him in a few minutes.

As he waited he admired the room, the tasteful decor, the hundreds of books, the original paintings. His appreciation was interrupted by the lady's entrance. He complimented her on her beautiful home saying, "You must be both deeply grateful and very happy to be blessed with a home like this."

Without a word she walked to a beautiful desk and took out a small, pearl-handled pistol. Laying it on the desk she said, "Everything you find so beautiful is overshadowed by the emptiness inside of me. Only the love and respect I have for my family has prevented me from using this on myself."

The outward trappings of success are often a facade hiding a desperate lostness. Without Christ, the rich and successful, like the prostitutes and derelicts, ". . . [have] problems . . . so great . . . they [don't] know what to do or where to go for help. They [are] like sheep without a shepherd" (Matt. 9:36 TLB).

Jesus was not contemptuous toward life's ragged rejects, nor was He in awe of this world's rich. To Him, everyone without God was a sheep without a shepherd, a sinner, lost and in need of a Savior.

HIS MISSION
Jesus asked, "What man of you, having a hundred sheep, if

he has lost one of them, does not leave the ninety-nine in the wilderness, and go after the one which is lost until he finds it?'' (Luke 15:4).

The analogy is obvious! The peril of the sheep and its value to the shepherd make a rescue effort imperative. Men are obviously more valuable than livestock. If a man will risk the dangers of the wilderness in search of his lost sheep, can't we expect God to brave the desolation and darkness of this world in search of lost men? If a shepherd leaves the ninety-nine to find the one lost sheep isn't it natural for Jesus to leave the company of the righteous and go into the wilderness of the wicked in search of the lost?

Concerning His mission, Jesus said: ". . . the Son of man came to seek and to save the lost'' (Luke 19:10) and ''Those who are well have no need of a physician, but those who are sick; I have not come to call the righteous, but sinners to repentance'' (Luke 5:31, 32).

Notice the shepherd's urgency. His concern for the lost sheep was so great that he left the ninety-nine sheep in the wilderness; his compulsion so acute that he left them on the mountains. There was no time to take them to the safety of the fold, night was falling, the lost sheep was in immediate danger.

When Leah, our daughter, was four we lived next to a large city high school. One afternoon as we were returning from grocery shopping we were forced to detour several blocks in order to get home, because the school was staging a parade to advertise its fall carnival. Leah was naturally fascinated by it and begged to be allowed to go to the corner and watch. We consented after giving her some stern instructions.

It probably didn't take more than five minutes to carry the groceries in but when I walked to the corner to find Leah, the parade was over and she was gone. I felt sick, scared. High school hot-rodders were burning up the street, oblivious to the crowds milling around and across the street. I pushed through the crowd, searching for her, calling her name. My imagination ran wild, picturing all sorts of things which could have happened to her.

Fear and concern drove me frantically on. I must have looked like a madman, pushing through the crowds, calling her name over and over again. After ten minutes of fruitless searching I ran home, hoping she had returned.

No such luck. Brenda and I decided on one more desperate search of the neighborhood before calling the police.

Such must have been the shepherd's sense of urgency as he left the ninety-nine and hurried into the mountains and wilderness in search of the one lost sheep. This same urgency is portrayed in the parable of the woman who lost one of her ten silver coins. She could not wait until morning but hurriedly lights a lamp and sweeps the house, searching diligently, until she finds it! (See Luke 15:8-10.)

Consider the persistence in each of these stories. Jesus uses almost the same words in both of them. He said the shepherd goes ". . . after the one which is lost, *until he finds it*" (Luke 15:4) and the woman searches ". . . diligently *until she finds it*" (Luke 15:8).

God cannot do less than these. He is the great shepherd and it is not His will that ". . . one of these little ones perish" (Matt. 18:14). Francis Thompson portrays this persistence well:

"I fled Him, down the nights and down the days;
I fled Him, down the arches of the years;
I fled Him, down the labyrinthine ways
Of my own mind; and in the midst of tears
I hid from Him, and under running laughter.
   Up vistaed hopes I sped;

And shot, precipitated,
Adown Titanic glooms of chasmed fears,
From those strong feet that followed, followed after.
But with unhurrying chase,
And unperturbed pace,
Deliberate speed, majestic instancy,
They beat—and a Voice beat
More instant than the Feet—
'All things betray thee, who betrayest Me.' ''[1]

The Psalmist said:

Whither shall I go from thy spirit? or whither shall I flee
from thy presence? If I ascend up into heaven, thou art
there: If I make my bed in hell, behold, thou art there. If I
take the wings of the morning, and dwell in the uttermost
parts of the sea; Even there shall thy hand lead me, and thy
right hand shall hold me. If I say, surely the darkness shall
cover me; even the night shall be light about me. Yea, the
darkness hideth not from thee; but the night shineth as the
day: the darkness and the light are both alike to thee.
(Ps. 139:7-12 KJV)

God will not cease His tireless efforts. His persistence is
unabated. He who came to seek and save the lost will not stop
until this day of grace is finally over.

When Brenda and I stepped out into the front yard to begin
one final frantic search, Leah was coming up the sidewalk, hand
in hand with the neighbor's teenage daughter. Our relief was
like a spasm causing our flesh to tremble and our legs to grow
weak. Our joy was enormous!

When the shepherd found his sheep he laid ''. . . it on his
shoulders, rejoicing. And when he [came] home, he [called]

[1]Francis Thompson, "The Hound of Heaven," (Fleming H. Revell Company, Westwood, New
Jersey, n.d.), p. 11.

73

together his friends and his neighbors, saying to them, 'Rejoice with me, for I have found my sheep which was lost' " (Luke 15:5, 6).

When the woman found her lost coin she called ". . . together her friends and neighbors, saying, 'Rejoice with me, for I have found the coin which I had lost' " (Luke 15:9).

When the prodigal returned, his father cried, " . . . Bring quickly the best robe, and put it on him; and put a ring on his hand, and shoes on his feet; and bring the fatted calf and kill it, and let us eat and make merry; for this my son was dead, and is alive again; he was lost and is found" (Luke 15:22-24).

Jesus said, "Just so, I tell you, there will be more joy in heaven over one sinner who repents than over ninety-nine righteous persons who need no repentance" (Luke 15:7).

HIS MINISTRY

The mission of Jesus is to seek and save the lost; He is the valiant shepherd braving the perils of the mountains and the wilderness in search of the lost sheep. In addition to His mission He also has a ministry. He not only saves the lost, but He ministers to the redeemed as well. He is the "good shepherd" who cares for His sheep.

Some months ago I received a phone call from a member of our church asking me to please visit her neighbor who was threatening suicide. As I drove toward her home I felt very limited in my own resources so I prayed earnestly for divine guidance and help.

As soon as we were seated I realized she was very distraught and I simply listened for the first forty-five minutes as she sobbed out her desperation. She had seen several psychiatrists, and spent some time in a psychiatric hospital without any significant results.

I asked her gently if she had ever tried God, if she would like to try Him now.

After several minutes of silence, in which she endured an enormous inner struggle, she said, "I don't think God will hear me."

"Why?" I asked.

"For years I didn't believe in Him or if I did I blamed Him for everything bad that happened to me. I've blasphemed Him. I've screamed at Him, I've called Him names."

Assuring her that He still loved her, I then read 2 Corinthians 5:17 about becoming a new creation when we trust in Christ and asked her if she wanted to pray and claim that promise. She nodded.

I placed the Bible, open to 2 Corinthians 5:17, on the table between us and asked her to put her hand on it to symbolize her acceptance of Christ. I then placed my hand on top of hers and instructed her to pray after me.

When we finished prayer I opened my eyes to a miracle. She was different. The desperation was gone. The deadness had left her eyes. She looked just bathed, peaceful. She kept smiling, repeating, "I feel so different."

The physical circumstances of her life were still difficult, her marriage was strained, she was separated from her son, financial problems were overwhelming, but she found the resources in Christ to cope successfully with those problems. She has continued to grow in the faith and is now one of our church school teachers.

The "good shepherd" not only found her in her lostness and brokenness but as the Psalmist said, He restored her soul. Moffatt's translation says, "He revives life in me. . . ." (Ps. 23:3), and for her it was a living experience!

This restoration, this reviving, is not so much an act as it is a relationship. When the shepherd in Jesus' story found the lost sheep he placed it on his shoulders and carried it home. I can almost see that emaciated sheep reviving as it absorbs the good shepherd's strength and vitality.

The shepherd not only restores the sheep to the flock but he provides for it. David wrote, "The Lord is my shepherd; I shall not want. . . . Thou preparest a table before me in the presence of mine enemies . . . my cup runneth over" (Ps. 23:1, 5). In John 10 Jesus identified Himself as the good shepherd and He said, "My purpose is to give life in all its fullness" (John 10:10).

And the good shepherd protects the sheep: "He who is a hireling and not a shepherd, whose own the sheep are not, sees the wolf coming and leaves them and flees; and the wolf snatches them and scatters them" (John 10:12); but ". . . the good shepherd lays down his life for the sheep" (John 10:11).

Life is demanding, filled with pitfalls and temptations. Our adversary the devil ". . . prowls around like a roaring lion, seeking some one to devour" (1 Pet. 5:8). The Living Bible says, ". . . looking for some victim to tear apart."

But we need not fear, for Jesus promises, "I am the good shepherd. The good shepherd lays down his life for the sheep" (John 10:11). Like David of old, ". . . I will fear no evil: for thou art with me; thy rod and thy staff they comfort ne" (Ps. 23:4 KJV).

The God of Grace

For the kingdom of heaven is like a householder who went out early in the morning to hire laborers for his vineyard. After agreeing with the laborers for a denarius a day, he sent them into his vineyard. And going out about the third hour he saw others standing idle in the market place; and to them he said, "You go into the vineyard too, and whatever is right I will give you." So they went. Going out again about the sixth hour and the ninth hour, he did the same. And about the eleventh hour he went out and found others standing; and he said to them, "Why do you stand here idle all day?" They said to him, "Because no one has hired us." He said to them, "You go into the vineyard too." And when evening came, the owner of the vineyard said to his steward, "Call the laborers and pay them their wages, beginning with the last, up to the first." And when those hired about the eleventh hour came, each of them received a denarius. Now when the first came, they thought they would receive more; but each of them also received a denarius. And on receiving it they grumbled at the householder, saying, "These last worked only one hour, and you have made them equal to us who have borne the burden of the day and the scorching heat."

But he replied to one of them, "Friend, I am doing you no wrong; did you not agree with me for a denarius? Take what belongs to you, and go; I choose to give to the last as I give to you. Am I not allowed to do what I choose with what belongs to me? Or do you begrudge my generosity?" So the last will be first, and the first last.

—Matt. 20:1-16

FOR years this parable has puzzled me, disturbed me. It seems so unfair, so out of character with the justice of God. My sympathies naturally gravitate toward those weary, sweat-streaked, sunburned men at the end of the line. And when I read how they received no more for twelve hours of labor than the denarius paid to those who only worked one hour, my sense of fair play is offended.

Were this unlikely drama to be re-enacted today would we not help file a grievance, call a strike, organize a union? Does not this owner's unexpected behavior irk us? But because this story is in the Bible, and because Jesus told it to reveal something about the character of God and the nature of His kingdom, we must work through our feelings and come to grips with this uncomfortable incident.

This parable can only be understood in the context of all the Scriptures. If this were the only reference we had concerning the personality and character of God we might draw some very unfavorable conclusions, but it is not, and the consensus of the Scriptures portrays God as good and just, faithful and loving. "O give thanks unto the Lord, for he is good . . ." (Ps. 107:1 KJV). ". . . Great and marvellous are thy works, Lord God Almighty; just and true are thy ways . . ." (Rev. 15:3 KJV).

And He does not change. If He was good in the Psalmist's day

He is still good, and if the revelator found Him just and true then, He still is. God is immutable!

". . . I am the Lord, I change not . . ." (Mal. 3:6 KJV).

Thou, Lord, didst found the earth in the beginning,
and the heavens are the work of thy hands;
they will perish, but thou remainest;
they will all grow old like a garment,
like a mantle thou wilt roll them up,
and they will be changed.
But thou art the same,
and thy years will never end. (Heb. 1:10-12)

". . . with whom there is never the slightest variation or shadow of inconsistency" (James 1:17 Phillips).

To understand this parable we must begin by believing the householder [God] is good. If His behavior rubs us the wrong way, let us understand that He is operating under the values of the kingdom of heaven. Don't try to judge His actions by earthly values, rather try to grasp the eternal values which form the basis of Jesus' story.

ADMIRABLE ATTRIBUTES

This householder is conscientious. He went into the market place early in search of laborers. Apparently he did not expect anyone to begin work before he did. His steward or some other trusted employee might have served as well to hire laborers, but he obviously cared enough to be personally involved.

We who work God's vineyard must never forget what a privilege is ours. We did not apply. God came into the disreputable market place of life and called us. "You did not choose me, but I chose you and appointed you that you should go and bear fruit and that your fruit should abide . . ." (John 15:16).

This does not mean that there are some that God rejects, some He does not choose, for He is ". . . not willing that any should perish, but that all should come to repentance" (2 Pet. 3:9). The householder went into the market place again and again, hiring all he could find, all who were willing to work.

Nor does the fact that all those he spoke to accepted employment mean that all men are going to be saved. In many other parables Jesus aptly portrays humanity's rebelliousness. When the king made a great banquet, those who were invited ". . . all alike began to make excuses" (Luke 14:18). There are other similar incidents: the unprofitable servant (Matt. 25), the foolish virgins (Matt. 25), the wicked husbandmen (Matt. 21), and many more which demonstrate mankind's unwillingness to accept God's forgiveness and fellowship.

The long day finally draws to a close, night descends and he makes no more trips to seek employees. All that remains is rewards for the laborers: "And when evening came, the owner of the vineyard said to his steward, 'Call the laborers and pay them their wages . . .' " (Matt. 20:8).

Make no mistake, this day of grace will end: He who has so patiently sought for lost men will finally cease His relentless efforts and those who have carelessly refused His grace shall be left alone in the dark night of desolation and " '. . . there men will weep and gnash their teeth' " (Matt. 25:30).

The owner's first trip to the market place can be attributed to his interest in seeing the vineyard worked. God expects production: "I am the true vine, and my Father is the vinedresser. Every branch of mine that bears no fruit, he takes away, and every branch that does bear fruit he prunes, that it may bear more fruit (John 15:1, 2). But his subsequent trips, at nine A.M., at noon, at three P.M., and finally at five P.M., suggest a deep interest in the laborers themselves.

Somewhere, I've long forgotten where, I read of the disillusionment and despair of workers on a government road crew during the depression in Ireland. It seems they discovered that the roads they were building went nowhere, just ended in impassable bogs. With this discovery came the realization that they were working only to give the government an excuse to feed them. Depression, life-draining, debilitating depression followed, for morale cannot survive when life has no purpose or meaning.

God understands this need for meaningful employment. Without it life has no purpose, no meaning, no direction. Everyone needs something to do, some place to be, someone to be responsible for. Nothing can so undermine a man's sense of self-worth as not being needed!

Reed is one of the most real people in the world. His weaknesses are limited almost entirely to impulsive acts of exaggerated generosity. He's never met a stranger, carries the needs of the world in his heart, and is on a first-name basis with the Lord!

Once, while preaching, he told how he would get up in the night to tend to his infant children. Sitting in a rocking chair, bottle-feeding a baby, he prayed for them, sang to them, loved them. As he shared the memory, wet tears ran down his craggy cheeks and many of us were touched by his tenderness and reached for handkerchiefs to dab our damp eyes. He finished his story by asking if we could think of anything worse than not being needed.

I can't! Can you?

Neither can God, and that's why Jesus has this householder making so many trips to the market place. It's not inaccurate to assume he hired a full crew his first time out, nor does it do the

Scriptures an injustice to say God's compassion for the unemployed is demonstrated by his repeated journeys. If God has every hair of our head numbered, knows when each tiny bird falls, personally clothes the grass (Luke 12), then it should not surprise us that He is concerned with the perils of unemployment, both economical and emotional.

His interest in the real world of physical needs does not at all mean that this parable is limited to that context. Jesus is revealing God's priorities to us. These men were hired, not so much because the householder needed them, but because they needed the job. God chooses us, not because He needs us, but because we so desperately need him.

God does not need our intercessory prayers to motivate Him to save the lost. He who gave His only Son has proved His desire and willingness. Intercessory prayer is for our benefit. We need it to put us in touch with His great heart and to allow us a part in redemption's eternal work.

God does not need us to witness, to preach, to give. But He knows our enormous need so He calls us to work in His vineyard. Our efforts are the tools He uses; but, even as He uses us, His hands are shaping us to the likeness of Christ. Never forget, God's first purpose is to transform us into authentic persons. The first fruit He desires from those who labor in His vineyard is personal character growth (see Gal. 5:22, 23). When we live truly transformed lives the "works" of righteousness will be an inevitable consequence, the vineyard will be worked, but if we strive to do the "works" of God rather than simply yielding to His craftsmanship we thwart His priorities.

GOD'S GENEROSITY VERSUS MAN'S GOODNESS
The long day finally drew to a close; weary, sweat-streaked men trooped toward the pay booth. The steward called the

eleventh-hour employees first and undoubtedly there were some uneasy rumblings among those who had toiled the entire day, rumblings which quieted only when they realized those who were hired last were receiving a full day's pay. Logic reasoned that they who had worked the whole day would receive an equal additional amount. They were only too glad to be paid last if it meant more money.

When the steward gave them their pay they were shocked! ". . . they thought they would receive more; but each of them also received a denarius" (Matt. 20:10).

There were no uneasy murmurings this time. They made their displeasure known. " . . . They grumbled at the householder, saying, 'These last worked only one hour, and you have made them equal to us who have borne the burden of the day and the scorching heat' " (Matt. 20:11, 12).

It doesn't seem fair! Why did the householder pay those who only worked an hour the same as those who worked twelve hours? He explains his actions, saying, "Friend, I am doing you no wrong; did you not agree with me for a denarius?" (Matt. 20:13).

This is the key which unlocks the whole parable. The first group of laborers "agreed" with him for a denarius a day; they negotiated a contract. Everyone else he hired trusted his fairness. " . . . You go into the vineyard too, and whatever is right I will give you . . ." (Matt. 20:4).

Negotiated contracts are an unquestioned necessity in the greedy business world but they have no place between God and man. If we insist that God be fair with us, if we demand that He "agree" to a contract, He will, but we are the losers. Left to His own desires He will always do what's right. Never forget, His mercy is always greater than our merit, His generous grace always exceeds our earned goodness. If we leave the choice to

Him, His great heart will always give us more than we deserve or could ever earn!

This parable is an object lesson in grace. The unhappy laborers were right when they said, ". . . you have made them equal to us . . ." (Matt. 20:12). The penitent malefactor received as much paradise (Luke 23:41-43) as the most innocent convert.

David Redding said it well when he wrote, ". . . God passes out the same salvation to us all. Heaven is heaven no matter who goes there or when. When a man comes to himself, whether it is as a prodigal son or on his deathbed, he goes home to the same Father. The penitent thief on the cross got as big a piece of paradise as innocent Joan of Arc. His penalty was his past—the time he put in hell while away in the far country."[1]

No man can brag about making it to heaven, ". . . it is the gift of God . . ." (Eph. 2:8). What "works" of righteousness the most conscientious and Christ-like do are inconsequential in comparison to the grace of God. "But drops of grief can ne'er repay the debt of love I owe; Here, Lord, I give myself away; 'Tis all that I can do."[2]

The Scriptures teach us to be grateful for the opportunity to suffer and labor for Christ. "And they departed from the presence of the council, rejoicing that they were counted worthy to suffer shame for his name" (Acts 5:41 KJV). If we ". . . have borne the burden of the day and the scorching heat . . ." (Matt. 20:12) we should be thankful for the opportunity to express our love, but often we aren't. We act as if we are doing God a favor and are quick to bill Him for our piddling acts of goodness. What audacity!

These impertinent laborers dare to challenge the owner's right to do with his money as he wishes and are soundly rebuked for their efforts. ". . . I am doing you no wrong. . . . Am I not

[1]David A. Redding, "The Parables He Told," (Fleming H. Revell Company, Westwood, New Jersey, n.d.), p. 32.
[2]Isaac Watts and Ralph E. Hudson, "At the Cross" in "Hymns of Glorious Praise," (Gospel Publishing House, Springfield, Mo., 1969), p. 84.

allowed to do what I choose with what belongs to me? Or do you begrudge my generosity?'' (Matt. 20:13-15).

One can only marvel at humanity's audaciousness. We who cannot maintain world peace, balance the national budget, wipe out world poverty or solve the racial crisis still think nothing of telling God how to run things. ''But who are you, a man, to answer back to God? Will what is molded say to its molder, 'Why have you made me thus?' '' (Rom. 9:20). ''Am I not allowed to do what I choose with what belongs to me?'' (Matt. 20:15).

Yet, grace does not mean God indiscriminately bestows His blessings, ''For the grace of God that bringeth salvation hath appeared to all men'' (Titus 2:11 KJV). It simply defines the way men must approach God and receive from Him. Nor does it mean we all shall receive the same wage at the end of life's day. It's a new way of measuring men based not just on what they did but on what they could have done. '' . . . Truly, I say to you, this poor widow has put in more than all those who are contributing to the treasury. For they all contributed out of their abundance; but she out of her poverty has put in everything she had, her whole living'' (Mark 12:43, 44).

In another place Jesus says, '' . . . Every one to whom much is given, of him much will be required; and of him to whom men commit much they will demand the more'' (Luke 12:48).

Those of us who were born to Christian parents, who cut our teeth on the gospel, who have been spared much of the temptation suffered by those less fortunate than we, are going to be expected to put in a fuller day in the vineyard. David Redding says, '' . . . God pays not on the basis of volume of work we have accomplished, but on the spirit in which we did what we could. Men will be paid not for what they did, so much as for

what they would have done if they had had the chance . . ."³
Grace rewards, not so much our success, but our obedient
efforts.

Obviously there's something terribly wrong in the hearts of
these day-long laborers. The very fact that they react with
indignation is a dead giveaway. They've worked his vineyard
but they've missed the point. They know nothing of their
employer's great heart; they're so interested in earning a wage
that they miss His interest in them. To them it's just another
day's work, a job, a paycheck, and they cheat themselves out of
His fellowship and misunderstand the reason for their
employment.

They seem oblivious to the fact that few have the sacred
privilege of spending life's entire day in His service, that few
are spared the lonely desperation of the spiritually unemployed.
They are obviously self-serving and greedy, without
compassion, and they end up playing the part of the prodigal's
older brother, " . . . Look, how many years have I slaved for
you and never disobeyed a single order of yours, and yet you
have never given me so much as a young goat so that I could
give my friends a dinner! But when this son of yours arrives,
who has spent all your money on prostitutes, for *him* you kill the
fatted calf!" (Luke 15:29-31 Phillips).

Don't be fooled by their injured act of innocence. They
received what they asked for, what they agreed to. " . . .
Friend, I am doing you no wrong . . ." (Matt. 20:13). Theirs
was not a service of love, but a calculating business deal in
which they trusted their own works, and now they are offended
when the landlord's generosity equally blesses those who toiled
only an hour.

Jesus told this entire story in response to a calculating question
by Peter. " . . . Lo, we have left everything and followed
³Redding, "The Parables He Told," p. 33.

you. What then shall we have?'' (Matt. 19:27). With His answer He challenges us to examine our motives. He promises great rewards, a hundredfold, thrones, eternal life; but He ends on a sober note, ''. . . many that are first will be last, and the last first'' (Matt. 19:30). Which is to say if we follow Him for such rewards and not out of love we will undoubtedly be disappointed in the end when some unassuming disciple is received first.

Our true motives are most clearly revealed by our reactions to the successes of others, particularly those who seem less deserving than we. If we truly rejoice in their blessings, then perhaps we are serving God and man out of a true heart of love. But if we resent God's blessings on their lives then we must pray for more grace and more Christ-likeness, for only pride and self-centeredness can cause us to begrudge the generosity of God's spirit toward another. Only blindness to our lifelong benefits can make us holler ''foul'' when God is good to the poor beggars who struggle home just under the wire.

The God Who Loves

And as they were eating, he took the bread, and blessed, and broke it, and gave it to them, and said, "Take; this is my body." And he took a cup, and when he had given thanks he gave it to them, and they all drank of it. And he said to them, "This is my blood of the covenant, which is poured out for many. Truly, I say to you, I shall not drink again of the fruit of the vine until that day when I drink it new in the kingdom of God."

—Mark 14:22-25

Jesus, knowing that the Father had given all things into his hands, and that he had come from God and was going to God, rose from supper, laid aside his garments, and girded himself with a towel. Then he poured water into a basin, and began to wash the disciples' feet, and to wipe them with the towel with which he was girded. . . . When he had washed their feet, and taken his garments, and resumed his place, he said to them, "Do you know what I have done to you? You call me Teacher and Lord; and you are right, for so I am. If I then, your Lord and Teacher, have washed your feet, you also ought to wash one another's feet. For I have given you an example, that you also should do as I have done to you. Truly, truly, I say to you, a servant is not greater than his master; nor is he who is sent greater than he who sent him. If you know these things blessed are you if you do them."

—John 13:3-5, 12-17

And they brought him to the place called Golgotha (which means the place of a skull). And they offered him wine mingled with myrrh; but he did not take it. And they crucified him, and divided his garments among them, casting lots for them, to decide what each should take. And it was the third hour when they crucified him. And the inscription of the charge against him read, "The King of the Jews."

—Mark 15:22-26

SOME time ago while browsing in a gift shop I came across a beautiful card. It was a soft-focus picture of a young woman standing on a cliff watching the surf pound the rocks below. Her hair was freely blowing in the wind and in the background a twisted and gnarled tree was visible. The caption, in Old English script, read, "Everything in this world changes except my love."

I was tempted to buy it for Brenda, but as I stood there, I realized my love was not unchanging. It was like the surf beating the rocks, influenced by storms and heavy winds. Like the rocks, it was worn and shaped by the constant rubbing. Putting the card back, I looked for one more honestly reflective of my deep, but still very human, love.

Several days later I accepted an invitation to speak at a Sweetheart Banquet. As I gave myself to preparation I found my mind still filled with the incident. Human love, I concluded, was variable; as subject to wear as the candy and cards, flowers and jewelry we use to express it.

Divine love—God's love—is unchanging, unchangeable, everlasting. Its symbols, common but unchanging: a loaf of bread, broken, and a cup of wine, a basin of water and a towel, two rough hewn timbers crudely fastened together—a cross.

BREAD AND WINE—LOVE GIVING

The true measure of love is not what we feel, or what we say, but what we give. When God commands us to love Him with all of our heart, mind, soul and strength and our neighbor as ourself (Matt. 22:36-39) He is not asking for an emotion, or a poetic declaration; rather He desires an act of self-giving, for more than anything else, love is the gift of oneself.

We know God's love is sincere because He gave and we know it is unlimited, infinite, immeasurable because He gave His best, His only begotten Son. ". . . the proof of God's amazing love is this: that it was while we were sinners that Christ died for us" (Rom. 5:8, Phillips). Someone has appropriately said, "When Christ died on the cross, God's pockets were empty." In Christ He gave all!

When Christ gave the bread and wine to the disciples He was re-enacting His incarnation and His life. He prophesied His imminent end, His bloody death. ". . . he took bread, and blessed, and broke it, and gave it to them, and said, 'Take; this is my body.' And he took a cup, and when he had given thanks he gave it to them, and they all drank of it. And he said to them, 'This is my blood of the covenant, which is poured out for many' " (Mark 14:22-24).

As we receive the communion we remember His great love, revealed through the gift of Himself. "Greater love has no man than this, that a man lay down his life for his friends" (John 15:13). "Rings and jewels," as Ralph Waldo Emerson said, "are not gifts but apologies for gifts. The only gift is a portion of thyself."

Jesus held back nothing, freely gave of Himself, totally. "I am the good shepherd. The good shepherd lays down his life for the sheep. . . . I lay down my life. . . . No one takes it from me, but I lay it down of my own accord . . ." (John 10:11, 17, 18).

At times I find myself especially vulnerable to His love and at those times I am almost overwhelmed with my need to love Him back, to somehow pay Him back. Herbert Tarr has described an emotional parting which is expressive of my feelings and also of God's, I believe. He writes:

The conductor called, "All visitors off the train!" "Oh, David. . . ." She hugged him to her bosom which smelled of fruits and vegetables and a mother's love. "Take care of him." These last words were addressed not to Uncle Asher nor even to the conductor, but to God. Tante Dvorah spoke to Him freely and often, for the Lord, to her way of thinking, was a person-sitter to whom loved ones were safely entrusted, as well as her senior partner in the business of living, always accessible and invariably amenable to petitions of love.

David looked at his aunt and uncle—she, with hands chapped and hard from selling fruit and vegetables outdoors in all kinds of weather, the face ruddy and round and invariably smiling, the heavy body more accustomed to a half a dozen sweaters at one time than a single coat, the hair the color of moonlight now, but the dark eyes still bright; he with his slight wiry body strong and bent from lifting too many fruit and vegetable crates for too many years, the wind-burned skin, the swarthy face impassive, except for the wry mouth—the childless couple who had taken the orphaned David into their home, rearing him since the age of seven yet refusing to be called "Mama" and "Papa" for fear that he would forget his real parents.

David grabbed their rough peddlers' hands in his smooth student ones. "How can I ever begin to pay you two for

what you've done for me!'' Uncle Asher spoke gently:
"David, there's a saying: 'The love of parents goes to their
children, but the love of these children goes to their
children.' ''

"That's not so!'' David protested, "I'll always be
trying to—'' Tante Dvorah interrupted, "David, what
your uncle Asher means is that a parent's love isn't to be
paid back; it can only be passed on.''[1]

When I am especially aware of God's love no task seems
impossible, no distance too far, no cost too high, no sacrifice
too great. I hear myself praying, "I'll pay you back, Lord,
somehow, even if it takes my whole life.'' And when I'm
especially sensitive to His nearness I hear Him say, "My love
isn't to be paid back; it can only be passed on.''

When God chose to express His love He became flesh,
became a man, lived among us. He shared His love, Himself, by
breaking the eternal bread of life and giving it to needy men. If
we, who have partaken of His love, would pass it on, we must
give of ourselves as He did. We must become a living
communion, broken bread distributed to the hungry, wine
poured out for life's thirsty.

A BASIN OF WATER AND A TOWEL—LOVE SERVING

My first pastorate was in a small rural community and the
church had a history of difficulties. I went to Holly armed with a
youthful naivete, believing things would be different under my
ministry. They weren't. And in a matter of months the recurring
difficulties, fed by jealousy and pettiness, were threatening to
prematurely terminate my call.

I prayed, as only the desperate can, and it seemed God was
leading me to have a foot-washing service. Like Jacob, I

[1]Herbert Tarr, quoted in "Creative Brooding," (The Macmillan Company, New York, Collier-
Macmillan Limited, London, 1966), p. 102.

wrestled with the Lord. My childhood memories of foot washings were vague, drab and uninspiring, seemingly unrelated to the present problems. Still His urgings remained, increased almost daily as I continued to seek His guidance. Finally surrendering, I scheduled the service for the following Sunday night.

Service time arrived, and I found myself facing nine stern men. As I stood to speak, feelings of foolishness and weakness swept over me, I wanted to run, to disappear. Breathing a desperate prayer I began, "Some of you feel I've played favorites, that I haven't ministered to your families like I should. You may be right, but I want you to know that if I have wronged you I did it ignorantly, out of inexperience, and not maliciously."

There was no visible response so I plunged on, "As a demonstration of my sincere desire to serve you and your family, in any way, great or small, I'm going to wash your feet."

Instructing them to remove their shoes and socks I rolled up my shirt sleeves and reached for the towel and the basin of water. There were some uneasy murmurings, but I ignored them and knelt before the nearest man. I apologized for any wrong I might have done and asked his forgiveness. Then I washed his feet, pledging to serve him faithfully in Christ's name.

As I moved from man to man something was happening. Bitterness and resentment, anger and grudges were being washed away. A sense of understanding and brotherhood filled the room, drew us together.

The effect of that service was revolutionary. The next two years were marked by progress in all areas of the church. There were problems and difficulties, to be sure, but that basin of water and towel provided the insights and attitudes to handle them creatively.

By taking a towel and a basin of water, by getting down on my knees, by washing their feet and apologizing, I had disarmed them. I had taken the fuse out of the time bomb of their anger. When I humbled myself and became vulnerable, when I placed myself in their hands, at their mercy, I appealed to all the love and goodness in their hearts.

No longer was I someone to resist. The spiritual dictator making demands and giving directions was gone and in his place was a servant volunteering to make life more meaningful in any way he could.

This idea was not original, the strategy not new. "For he, who had always been God by nature, did not cling to his privileges as God's equal, but stripped himself of every advantage by consenting to be a slave by nature and being born a man" (Phil. 2:6,7, Phillips).

He ". . . rose from supper, laid aside his garments, and girded himself with a towel. Then he poured water into a basin, and began to wash the disciples' feet, and to wipe them with the towel with which he was girded" (John 13:4, 5).

With this unpretentious act Christ left us His strategy for ministry, His way of sharing love. No deep philosophy, no heavy theology, no glib phrases, just a humble gesture of service. A willingness to be used. "He who is the greatest among you shall be your servant . . ." (Matt. 23:11).

I heard Arthur Katz, a converted Jew, share his testimony and he told of becoming so disillusioned with life that at age thirty-four he found himself living out of a rucksack as he hitchhiked around the world. One morning, while hitchhiking in Switzerland, he was picked up by a vivacious Christian man who treated him like an exalted guest.

The stranger was such a good listener that Art found himself pouring out his life story—his Jewishness, his cynicism, his brokenness and his desperation. He confessed that he was searching for life's meaning. The driver listened with such love that it seemed he absorbed Art's pain and brokenness into his own life, helping him bear it.

When Art finally finished the man asked, "Do you know what the world needs?" Art's defenses came up immediately and he prepared to debate. "The world needs for men to wash one another's feet." The response was so unexpected that Art was speechless. Then he had a vision of all the proud, arrogant people in the world on their knees washing each other's feet. Suddenly, for the first time, Christianity made sense, the brotherhood of man was a tangible possibility. Shortly thereafter Art became a Christian.

What philosophy, intellectualism, and debate couldn't do, love did! By listening, the man had figuratively washed Art's feet. His attitude of loving service disarmed Art, left him susceptible to the presence of Christ.

The world is full of people like Art: people who are hurting, people who are crying to be loved. Let's respond with a towel and a basin of water, by gently washing the dust of despair from their bruised souls. Remember, Christ on His knees washing feet is our example and God's definition of love serving.

A CROSS—LOVE SAVING

The cross is God's message of love to a lost world. Not His first word of love, nor His only word, but His best! He spoke a word of love from Bethlehem's manger, ". . . Emmanuel (which means, God with us)" (Matt. 1:23). Angels announced, "For to you is born this day in the city of David a Savior, who is Christ the Lord" (Luke 2:11). But man misunderstood the message from the manger, thought He was just another baby, forgot the angels and other unusual events in the dreary busyness of daily living.

God tried again; He spoke clearly through the miracles of Jesus. But still men misunderstood. Those who loved Him thought He was ". . . John the Baptist . . . Elias . . . Jeremias, or one of the prophets" (Matt. 16:14 KJV). His enemies accused Him of performing miracles by the power of Beelzebul, the prince of demons.

Finally God spoke through the cross. He wrote His love message on the trembling tissues of Christ's suffering flesh and hung it on the cross for all the world to see. What pen and ink on parchment could never say, God clearly said with iron spikes, broken flesh and spilled blood!

> While we were yet weak . . . Christ died for the ungodly. Why, one will hardly die for a righteous man—though perhaps for a good man one will even dare to die. But God shows his love for us in that while we were yet sinners Christ died for us. (Rom. 5:6-8)

The cross is not only God's message of love but of salvation as well. Christ on the cross is love saving!

Some months ago a young man came to my office for counsel. It was a bitterly cold December night but the winter chill was nothing compared to the frozen hopelessness in his manner. In an emotionless way, which was more painful to behold than expressed anxiety, he bitterly catalogued his failures and sins. Drug abuse, alcoholism, unfaithfulness. He finished by saying his wife had served him with divorce papers.

Gently I told him of God's love and the great lengths He went to express it and to provide forgiveness for people just like him. We knelt and prayed together and as he sobbed out his confession, the Holy Spirit made him born again.

He left, still ashamed and hurting, but forgiven and with new hope. In the weeks which followed God restored his marriage, and his wife and children joined him as faithful worshipers.

The cross is the pledge of God's willingness to love. Paul testifies, ". . . Christ Jesus came into the world to save sinners . . ." (1 Tim. 1:15). It is evidence of His sufficiency, that "He is able to save completely all who come to God through him . . ." (Heb. 7:25 TLB).

The songwriter said so appropriately:

There is a fountain filled with blood,
drawn from Immanuel's veins;
And sinners plunged beneath that flood,
Lose all their guilty stains.

The dying thief rejoiced to see,
That fountain in his day;
And there may I, though vile as he,
Wash all my sins away.[2]

Following worship one Sunday morning the pastor found a scrap of paper between the pews. Someone had written, with a crayon in childish scrawl, "Do you love me?"

Isn't that what we're all asking? Aren't human needs basically the same the world over? Don't we all need to be loved, and forgiven, and cared for? Isn't this why we go to church, to find out if God loves us?

God answers, with broken bread and wine, with a basin of water and a towel, and most eloquently with His son on a cross. On the cross, Jesus spreads His arms out wide and answers, "World, I love you big, this much!"

[2]William Cowper, "There is a Fountain Filled with Blood," in "Hymns of Glorious Praise," (Gospel Publishing House, Springfield, Missouri, 1969), p. 95.

Wally Armbruster records an imagined conversation:

" 'Hey man, you say you're gonna let your son go down there? He could get killed.'

'Maybe.'

'That's dangerous. They got knives and guns. They steal and get drunk and . . . man, he could get killed.'

'Maybe he could do some good.'

'Yeah, yeah. He'll go down there and try to help and they'll laugh at him.'

'Prob'ly so.'

'You can't love your son very much.'

'As much as anybody else. I love him a whole lot.'

'Yet you'd let him take a chance with losing his life for a bunch of niggers and poor people and people with no education . . . people you don't even know and don't know you or him and act like enemies of society and America and everything that's right. You love him, baloney. He could *die*.'

'There are worse things than dying for something you believe in.'

'Like what?'

'Like staying alive and having nothing you believe in enough to take a chance on dying for it.'

'Man, that's all right in theory. But this is your son. He's got to be more important than anything or anybody . . . or else you don't amount to much as a father. You're cold.'

'And so he did go. I let him go because he wanted to. And I wanted him to. He didn't do much good there. Oh, he won a few followers . . . a handful of fishermen and some others, plus a lot of people who weren't exactly against him but were not willing to get involved when it got right down to the die-for-it bit. And the guy was right. They did kill him. Put him on a cross. My son.' ''[3]

And that's truly love saving.

[3]Wally Armbruster, "A Bag of Noodles," (Concordia Publishing House, St. Louis, Missouri, 1972), p. 7.

Though He Slay Me

"Though he slay me, yet will I trust him. . . ."
—Job 13:15 (KJV)

L EAH, our seven-year-old daughter, was sick for just over a week some months ago. The doctor was not overly concerned; he prescribed penicillin to combat her strep throat condition and instructed us to give her aspirin to keep her fever down, and plenty of liquids. Nonetheless, it was a harrowing week for Brenda and me. Leah's throat swelled almost shut, giving her a rattling wheeze, and her head was so congested, breathing through her nose became impossible.

Brenda and I probably overreact to Leah's bouts with colds and flu, but I think our reaction is understandable in light of the severe illness she suffered when she was just a baby.

We took her to the doctor after two days of vomiting and while he was examining her she went into convulsions. After trying unsuccessfully for more than ten minutes to stop them, he called the hospital and told them to prepare for an emergency. The hospital was alerted and when we arrived Leah (still convulsing) was taken into a specially equipped emergency area, where a team of doctors and nurses labored for the next two and one-half hours to save her.

When she was finally brought out of the emergency room we almost didn't recognize her. She was clad only in a diaper, her hands and feet were fastened by cloth cords to the bars of the baby bed. Nutrients and medicines were flowing through tubes into a vein in her head.

Leah spent several days in the hospital and underwent a battery of tests. They failed to reveal anything and, since she was improving rapidly, the doctor released her after telling us he had absolutely no explanation for her illness and convulsions and that we should be very grateful she was alive.

Now each time Leah becomes sick, we wonder if something similar is in the making. We are frightened, not so much by the present illness, but by the possibility of what it might develop into. It is probably an irrational fear since Leah has run high fevers and been very sick several times since 1971 without the convulsions recurring a single time. Still, her latest illness produced a fearful week, and several nights I sat in the rocking chair in the living room holding her. She was feverish and wheezing. When she cried in discomfort I thought my heart would break. I felt so helpless. There was nothing more I could do and yet I felt like there should be. I prayed desperately for God to heal her and was tempted with anger when He didn't.

In the shadowy darkness of the night, I listened to Leah's ragged wheezing, and wondered what kind of a God would let an innocent child suffer so. I remembered John Claypool's book about his struggle as he watched his eight-year-old daughter, Laura Lue, suffer and die from leukemia. [1] I thought of Dennis Chambers, husband, and father of three, injured and facing back surgery. Another friend came to mind; he is a relatively young man in his late thirties and yet he has been sick and unable to work steadily for several years. The whole church has often prayed for his healing; still he remains sick and his family suffers financially and emotionally.

"Why?" my mind screamed into the darkness. "Why?" No answers came, at least none that my uneasy mind could grasp.

[1]John Claypool, "Tracks of A Fellow Struggler," (Word Books, Waco, Texas, 1975).

What are we to do when the darkness descends, smothering the light? When illness makes suffering and death a painful reality? When our faith is battered and beaten by the unrelenting winds of uncertainty and fear? When our prayers seem useless and our questions go unanswered?

We are faced with a choice: we can choose to trust God and His goodness or we can deny His very existence.

I choose to trust God, and make no mistake it is a choice, an act of my will. I choose to trust Him because the alternative, such as it is, offers only emptiness.

THE ALTERNATIVE

If we do not trust in the goodness and sovereignty of God, then we must believe, if we believe He exists at all, that He is cruel or incompetent. We hear ourselves blaming Him, saying with the slave George Harris of *Uncle Tom's Cabin,* "They buy and sell us and make trade of our heart's blood and groans and tears, and God lets them, He does; God lets them!"

And if we choose to believe there is no God, then life is reduced to cliché; a senseless tragedy directed by an idiot. Without God, life is robbed of its reason, reduced to a frustrating, meaningless treadmill. Without Him we are left alone, not only without any answers, but without His presence to trust when there are no answers.

Some may ask, "Isn't that better? Those who don't even try to believe seem to be spared much pain and disappointment. They seem capable of accepting life at face value, of taking happiness where they find it."

If the absence of uncertainty and pain is life and happiness, then perhaps the answer is yes. But if real life and meaningfulness is creativity in the midst of conflict, then the answer must be no. Emphatically no!

Arthur Gordon discusses this when he writes:

". . . when things are going pretty well at last, and the pressure is off, and you're not frightened any more, sometimes you look back. You look back at all the misery and uncertainty, at the times when it was really rough, when you didn't think you could keep going for another day or even another hour. You expect to feel a great relief.

"But you don't. You feel a kind of sadness—almost a sort of regret—a sense of loss rather than gain. Because you begin to realize that those times—grim though they were—had a vividness, a reality far more intense than the easier present. And it takes only a word, or a gesture, or a few notes from an old song to bring it all flooding back. . . ."[2]

And how real is the apparent happiness of those who deny the existence of God? What are they really like when they're alone? When illness becomes a terminal reality? When they stand at the graveside of their young child?

I suspect it is a façade, a thin veneer stretched across an aching emptiness. Do they not feel something of the loss expressed by the prominent scientist who said, ". . . when I think about my loss of faith I experience the sharpest pain of which my nature is capable."

Are not many of them like Jack London, Ernest Hemingway, and other literary idols who apparently found life and meaning without God, yet in the end took their own lives, proving how shallow and cheap life without God really is?

This past week I was called upon to preach a funeral and as I was preparing, I asked myself what I would do if something happened to Leah, if Brenda suddenly died or was killed. I allowed the possibility to take shape in my mind, I rolled it around trying to imagine the sorrow and sense of loss, trying to perceive the implications and far-reaching impact. My

[2]Arthur Gordon, "A Touch of Wonder" (Fleming H. Revell Company, Old Tappan, New Jersey, 1974), p. 35.

conclusions are only speculative, but I decided that God would be sufficient to sustain me in my sorrow and able to make life meaningful again.

Then I found myself asking what I would do if something happened to God? It was the most sobering thought I have ever experienced, and I realized in the deepest possible way how truly dependent I am on Him. Life without Leah would have something missing, life without Brenda would be burdensome, but life without God would be impossible! If something happened to God, if He were gone, I couldn't go on living.

So I choose to trust Him, to believe in His goodness. Sometimes it's a difficult choice, faced with the tragedy and turmoil which is so much a part of every day, but for me it's the only one. Anything else would be emotional, spiritual, and, very possibly, physical suicide.

TRUST

Trusting God gives order and meaning to life. That is not to say we suddenly are able to decode all of life's painful riddles, but that decoding becomes unnecessary. We do not have to understand, we simply believe God has everything under control, that in His own good time He will reveal how each incident was fitted into His ultimate plan. Not that He willed such things as sickness and war, but that He was able to use even such tragedies as instruments for good.

Some time ago I read an autobiography entitled *Joni*.[3] It was the account of a young woman's struggle to understand, accept and adjust to total paralysis from the neck down, which resulted from a diving accident she suffered at age seventeen. Today she is an accomplished artist (she draws with her mouth and teeth) whose works are exhibited across the United States, and a dynamic and effective witness for our Lord.

[3]Joni Eareckson with Joe Musser, "Joni," (Zondervan Publishing House, Grand Rapids, Michigan, 1976).

Her story is painful and real, honestly expressing her desperate struggle with anger, bitterness, despair and thoughts of suicide. She attained trust in God only after several abortive beginnings, but once realized it transformed her into a vivacious Christian.

Her trust was developed slowly and painfully. For a time it seemed necessary to intellectually understand how her accident was working "together for good. . ." (Rom. 8:28 KJV). She wondered if this was punishment for lust and self-centeredness. Was the "good" her heavenly Father wanted to give her (Matt. 7:11) the use of her hands, total healing, a loving Christian husband who was capable of coping with her handicap? As each of these expectations proved to be false she was forced more and more into an unquestioning trust in God.

Once she was able to accept her condition, even though she couldn't intellectually explain how God was using it for good, she found freedom from bitterness and self-pity. God then began to open doors and move her into a real ministry reaching literally millions.

Some of the "good" He was working is now obvious, some of it we won't know until eternity. I cannot believe God caused Joni's accident; perhaps He allowed it. For certain He took advantage of it, He used it!

For me, trusting God means believing that He will utilize every incident to work His will in my life. This disarms disaster, for what can overwhelm us if we believe God will turn it to our advantage?

Joseph was sold into slavery by his jealous brothers but God exalted him to the second most powerful man in Egypt and Joseph said, when he confronted his brothers, ". . . ye thought evil against me; but God meant it unto good, to bring to pass, as it is this day, to save much people alive" (Gen. 50:20 KJV).

Paul was imprisoned, but God used it to inspire him to write much of the New Testament. Paul himself acknowledged the hand of God in it, when he said, "I want you to know, brethren, that what has happened to me has really served to advance the gospel. . ." (Phil. 1:12).

Such trust is possible only when we believe unquestioningly in the loving goodness and eternal competence of God. Then when life reduces us to virtual helplessness we can trust God without recourse to intellectual understanding or comprehension. We can survive and triumph by believing that God has things under control and that ". . . our light affliction, which is but for a moment, worketh for us a far more exceeding and eternal weight of glory. . ." (2 Cor. 4:17 KJV).

For the past year I have been ministering to a couple who are living under extreme duress. He is out on bond awaiting trial on two counts of sexual assault on his wife's seventeen-year-old daughter. Stipulations on the bond have prevented him from living at home and his wife has been unable to control the teenage children, resulting in several violent and disorderly incidents which precipitated their removal to foster homes. Both he and she have been married previously and have been involved for years in alcoholic situations; she by marriage and he as an alcoholic since he was a teenager. Their lives are literally scarred and twisted by sin.

They have been a part of our congregation for the last year and during that time several of the members have remarked to me that they do not know how Jane and Sterling bear up under it so well. I tell them they are able to do it because they have learned to trust God.

They are not living with any false hopes. They know prison is a very real possibility and they are aware of the dangers for a sex offender in the penitentiary. Still, they have both experienced the best year of their lives. God is their salvation and their sufficiency. They believe He will use whatever happens to their good, and they know He will not allow them to "... be tempted beyond [their] strength, but with the temptation will also provide the way of escape. . . " (1 Cor. 10:13).

Without God their lives would have been filled with bitterness and hatred; instead they have become an integral part of our local church and a source of strength and inspiration to many.

It's easier to trust God when we realize He has faced similar temptations and life situations. Christ can truly understand Joni's paralysis and the accompanying helplessness, for wasn't He "paralyzed" while He hung on the cross. He couldn't even quench His own thirst, but had to depend on others to give Him a drink (John 19:28-30).

Jesus knows what Sterling feels when he is tried in court, for He experienced two trials before His execution; one before Caiaphas and the Sanhedrin and the other a civil trial before Pontius Pilate the governor. He experienced the loneliness of the accused and the sense of helplessness which is an inevitable part of having one's future in the hands of another.

He too suffered in the darkness, without light and without answers. He felt totally alone, abandoned by God. ". . . My God, my God, why hast thou forsaken me?" (Mark 15:34). But no answer came. Nothing but those poignant words bouncing around in the darkness, echoing with emptiness, haunting and mocking him.

Though alone in the dark, apparently abandoned by all, God included, He did not curse and die shamed and doubting. He endured, trusting, until the darkness eased a little and His suffering made some sense. Faith found its voice and acknowledged the purpose of it all, even the darkness, saying,

". . . It is finished. . ." (John 19:30). Trust increased until we see Him face death with assurance. "Father, into thy hands I commit my spirit!" (Luke 23:47).

There is no life experience, no pain, no silence, no darkness that He does not understand. "For we have not a high priest who is unable to sympathize with our weaknesses, but one who in every respect has been tempted as we are, yet without sinning" (Heb. 4:15). And ". . . because he himself has suffered and been tempted, he is able to help those who are tempted" (Heb. 2:18).

If we trust Him and lean upon Him we can face temptation without failing; but if we do fail He is able to take those failures and use them as tools which contribute to our final Christ-likeness.

My grandmother did a lot of what she called "handiwork." Included in that catch-all phrase was crocheting, knitting, embroidering and quilting. Quilting was my favorite because I was always amazed at how she could take all the discarded scraps and fashion them into a beautiful, symmetrical, multicolored masterpiece.

Trust enables me to see God like that. My life is often bits and pieces, seemingly unrelated scraps, but I know God is making them all work together for my ultimate good and when He is finally finished, the quilt of my life will be a sanctified tapestry reflecting His faithfulness.

Jesus—God's Idea of Himself

In the beginning was the Word, and the Word was with God, and the Word was God. He was in the beginning with God; all things were made through him, and without him was not anything made that was made. . . . And the Word became flesh and dwelt among us, full of grace and truth; we have beheld his glory, glory as of the only Son from the Father. . . . No one has ever seen God; the only Son, who is in the bosom of the Father, he has made him known.

—John 1:1-3, 14, 18

God, who gave to our forefathers many different glimpses of the truth in the words of the prophets, has now, at the end of the present age, given us the truth in the Son. Through the Son God made the whole universe, and to the Son he has ordained that all creation shall ultimately belong. This Son, radiance of the glory of God, flawless expression of the nature of God, himself the upholding power of all that is, having effected in person the cleansing of men's sin, took his seat at the right hand of the majesty on high—thus proving himself, by the more glorious name that he had been given, far greater than all the angels of God.

—Heb. 1:1-4 (Phillips)

Now Christ is the visible expression of the invisible God. . . .

—Col. 1:15 (Phillips)

Yet it is in him (Christ) that God gives a full and complete expression of himself in bodily form.

—Col. 2:9 (Phillips)

" "THE story is told of a devout member of a Hindu sect who was confronted with the claims of Christ. To him all life was sacred—a cow, an insect, a cobra. Yet, he could not grasp the Christian concept that God actually visited this planet in the flesh in the person of Jesus of Nazareth, as we are told in John 1:14. One day as he walked through the fields wrestling in his mind with this concept of God, he observed also an ant hill with thousands of ants in evidence. He observed that the ant hill was in the path of a farmer plowing the field. Gripped with a concern that you and I would feel for hundreds of people trapped in a burning building, he wanted to warn them of their impending destruction. But how? He could shout to them, but they would not hear. He could write in the sand, but they would be unable to read. How then could he communicate with them? Then, the realization came. If only he were an ant, he could warn them before it was too late. Now, he understood the Christian concept. God became a man—Jesus Christ—in order to communicate His love and forgiveness to us."[1]

John writes, ". . . the Word [Christ] became flesh and dwelt among us . . ." (John 1:14) and He did communicate love and forgiveness. But to limit the purpose of His humanity to that is to do the incarnation a severe injustice. Jesus came, not so much

[1]William R. Bright, "A Teacher's Manual for The Ten Basic Steps Toward Maturity," (Campus Crusade for Christ International, Arrowhead Springs, San Bernardino, California, 1965), pp. 18, 19.

to speak God's message, but to be the "message," ". . . the flawless expression of the nature of God . . ." (Heb. 1:3, Phillips).

When God decided to reveal Himself, to make Himself known to the world, He gave us Christ. John declares the purpose of Christ to be the revelation of the unseen God, to make God known to men. Jesus told us of the Father as He knew Him, made Him familiar to us in His parables, with His word pictures, in His sermons, yet God was not really known or understood. Words, however eloquent, are only shadowy glimpses of God; only the "Word" can truly reveal God.

The teachings of Jesus are His idea of the Father. The "Word" made flesh, Jesus, is God's idea of Himself. His "Word" to the world about Himself! The Son is ". . . the flawless expression of the nature of God . . ." (Heb. 1:3). "Now Christ is the visible expression of the invisible God . . ." (Col. 1:15, Phillips), and ". . . it is in him that God gives a full and complete expression of himself . . ." (Col. 2:9, Phillips).

God is infinite, greater than all revelations of Himself, incapable of being completely comprehended by the finite minds of men. Christ was indeed ". . . the flawless expression . . ." of God but it is impossible for us to grasp the fullness of His revelation. Ours is a growing revelation, a piecing together of bits and pieces as we come to a fuller and fuller comprehension.

I am acutely aware of the incompleteness of my own understanding, I know I ". . . see and understand only a little about God . . . as if [I] were peering at [my] reflection in a poor mirror . . ." (1 Cor. 13:12 TLB). Still I would like to share some of the insights the "Word" has made known to me. A book, volumes of books, could not deal comprehensively with the revelation of God in Christ so I certainly do not presume to do so in one brief chapter. Here I offer only some insights which are especially meaningful to me at this time.

GOD IS DARING IN LOVE

Jesus is, by nature, God. Not one-third God, not a junior member of the Godhead, but God. "In the beginning was the Word, and the Word was with God, and the Word was God" (John 1:1). Philippians says, ". . . he . . . had always been God by nature . . ." (2:6, Phillips).

When the ". . . Word became flesh . . ." (John 1:14) He did not cease to be God, He simply became ". . . the visible expression of the invisible God" (Col. 1:15, Phillips). God in the flesh!

Yet by becoming a man Jesus did empty Himself. ". . . he did not cling to his equality with God but emptied himself to assume the condition of a slave, and become as men are . . ." (Phil. 2:6, 7, Jerusalem Bible).

Jesus the man was still "very God of very God." His self-emptying does not mean He gave up His divine nature. The Phillips Modern English translation says, ". . . [He] stripped himself of every advantage by consenting to be a slave by nature and being born a man" (Phil. 2:7).

By comparing verse seven in the Jerusalem Bible and in the Phillips Modern English, it is possible to understand that He emptied Himself of every advantage of His divine nature. That is to say, while He was a man on this earth He limited Himself to those resources which are available to all men. He was still God but His divine nature was completely dormant. He coped with life on the same terms as other men.

As a child growing up in the church, I was taught that Jesus could have changed His mind at any time, dropped His robe of flesh and reassumed His position as God's equal. I know of no Scripture to substantiate such an assumption and if it were indeed the case, then Jesus really didn't empty Himself of every advantage, nor was He really tempted as we are. If such an escape was always available to Him then He did not face life under the same limits as other men.

For the incarnation to be valid, for the humanity and temptations of Christ to be real, His manhood must be the result of an irrevocable choice. Once Jesus was born in Bethlehem only two possibilities remained. He could remain faithful, resist all temptation, fulfill His mission, become the Savior, and ascend to God, or He could sin and suffer the deadly consequences the same as other doomed men.

The real risks of the incarnation can be realized only to the degree that we understand Christ's capacity for failure and the accompanying consequences. To agree that Jesus would go to hell if He sinned is really not acknowledging any risks unless we understand that sinning was a very real possibility. And His potential for sinning is perceived only to the degree that we see Him as a real man, only to the degree that we understand His self-emptying and its possible ramifications.

Many believers mistakenly assume that Jesus always knew as much about Himself as we know about Him now. For instance, they assume He was born with the knowledge of who He was and why He was here. Yet if He had that kind of knowledge, how could the author of the epistle to the Hebrews claim He was tempted in all things like the rest of mankind (Heb. 4:15)? For Him to truly be human, as He claimed, He had to experience life like any other baby, and He did. He experienced, as Luke 2:52 indicates, the same emotional and physical developmental processes as other children.

What Jesus came to know concerning His uniqueness was

probably as the result of what Mary and Joseph shared with Him concerning His unusual birth. At twelve, rich with the faith and optimism of youth, it was relatively easy for Him to believe He was God's Son (Luke 2:49); but as He grew older the Scriptures seem to indicate that this became a sensitive spot, a vulnerable point where He experienced considerable temptation (Matt. 4:1-7). Still He came to believe firmly in His deity and made many references to His unique relationship with the Father. On the night He was betrayed the Scriptures reveal that He knew He came from God and was returning to God (John 13:3). Still, it should be understood that this knowledge was the result of prayerful intimacy, revelation from God, and scriptural understanding rather than any memory of His deity.

In the incarnation Christ's divine nature became dormant. He "emptied" Himself of all previous knowledge, all power and all memory. "It was imperative that he should be made like his brothers in every respect . . ." (Heb. 2:17, Phillips).

This means God was risking everything on a baby, a small boy, a teenager, a young man of limited exposure and education. Inherent in this risk was not only all humanity, but the "only begotten Son" as well.

Dying on the cross was not the real risk. It was part of the divine plan, ". . . he himself likewise partook of the same nature, that through death he might destroy him who has the power of death, that is the devil, and deliver all those who through fear of death were subject to lifelong bondage" (Heb. 2:14, 15). It was a painful strategy to be sure, and costly, but still it was part of the plan.

The real risks were the temptations, the misunderstandings, the pressure to conform, the loneliness in Gethsemane, the darkness from the sixth hour until the ninth. One mistake, one sin and it's all over. If Christ fails all is lost: the world, for there is no other sacrifice for sin (Heb. 10:26); Jesus, for the wages of sin is death (Rom. 6:23); and God, for if Jesus sinned wouldn't it mean God was guilty too?

Jesus was no less God while He was a man than before the incarnation; He was still "very God of very God." Since they are one, wouldn't Jesus' guilt become God's as well? If so wouldn't that be the defeat of God? Wouldn't sin and darkness reign? Wouldn't Satan rule in evil ingenuity? The possible ramifications are staggering!

I offer these possibilities only as a means of making us aware of the risks God so daringly took to make His love known and to secure our salvation. Many of us accept the incarnation, the temptations, the crucifixion, almost nonchalantly as if the risks were nonexistent, as if success was always a foregone conclusion. It wasn't, and the thirty-three years Christ spent on this planet were years of trial with all creation weighed in the balances, and stand now as an eternal testimony to God's daring love.

FAITHFUL IN LOVE

By recognizing the perils inherent in the incarnation we have taken the first step toward a fuller appreciation of God's gift. In this life we probably never will perceive their full extent, but we can increase our awareness by exploring some of the situations and temptations which Jesus may have faced.

Consider how difficult it must have been for Him to accept His deity. As it has already been pointed out, it was probably relatively easy as a boy, but it surely became more difficult as He approached manhood. Remember, He was a devout Jew and part of a monotheistic religious culture where such claims were blasphemy, punishable by death. One can only imagine the hours He spent agonizing over the Scriptures and in prayer as He tried to correlate the apparently contradictory issues of His life.

And then there must have been the whispered rumors about His birth. It is safe to assume that Mary and Joseph told no one of the virgin birth, and who would have believed them anyway? Yet Mary's condition must have been apparent at the time of the marriage, or at least grounds for strong speculation after Jesus was born. The Scriptures do clearly teach that His family origin was grounds for rejecting Him even after He began His ministry (see Mark 6:3 and John 9:29). How often He must have lain awake at night trying to decide if He was truly divine, the child of a virgin birth as His mother said, or if He was a "love child" as some of the more vicious wags suggested.

Tradition teaches that Joseph died, leaving Jesus to care for Mary and the other children. This responsibility possibly became another area of conflict and temptation. Early in His ministry, the Scriptures reveal that His brothers and His mother tried to convince Him to give up His madness and come home (see Mark 3:31). Is it possible that Mary lost her vision, grew comfortable and secure with Jesus in the small carpenter shop? Did she resist every effort He made to begin His ministry? Did Jesus speak out of His own painful experience when He told prospective disciples, "And a man's foes will be those of his own household" (Matt. 10:36)?

We know that Mary became one of His most committed followers, risking her own life to be near Him when He was crucified. We know she went early to the tomb that first Easter morning, that she was present in the upper room when the Holy Spirit came and that she was a pillar of strength in the early church, but we must not let this knowledge make us blind to the possible struggles which may have preceded her surrender, struggles which quite possibly involved Jesus.

What about His feelings of failure? Were there not possibly

times when He remembered the carpenter shop with real nostalgia, longed to be once again a part of its familiar routine? At times like when ". . . many of his disciples went back, and walked no more with him" (John 6:66 KJV). His " . . . Will ye also go away?" (John 6:67 KJV) is heavy with hurt and feelings of failure.

And His loneliness. Most of us assume that Jesus spent so much time in prayer because He was so spiritual, so devoted. He was, but several other considerations were included in His motivation, not the least of which was loneliness. He longed for intimacy with someone who understood Him, who shared His vision.

Even His closest disciples failed Him here. To Peter He said, ". . . thou savourest not the things that be of God . . ." (Matt. 16:23 KJV). To Philip, " . . . Have I been with you so long, and yet you do not know me, Philip?" (John 14:9).

Though famous and followed by thousands, though living with the twelve, He was still lonely. He heard things no one else heard, saw things no one else saw, felt things no one else felt and every effort to share these soul stirrings only aggravated His aloneness. Consequently He sought the fellowship of God in prayer and found in Him an understanding and sensitive confidant.

Then there's Gethsemane with its unapproachable and unfathomable agony. What trauma, what inner conflict, what doubt, what fear, can so rend a man that he sweat blood? Who can know the anguish which birthed our Lord's cry, " . . . My soul is very sorrowful, even to death . . ." (Mark 14:34).

And the darkness. A premature darkness which deformed the day, a thick death darkness, a heavy, hopeless, end-of-the-world darkness which came suddenly, without warning at noon, smothering the world. Then out of the darkness, pregnant with pain, ". . . Eloi, Eloi, lama sabachthani? . . . My God, my God, why hast thou forsaken me?" (Mark 15:34).

No one knows what Jesus suffered in the darkness, what pain forced that cry through His broken lips. Was God really gone or did Jesus just feel He was deserted? Did this sense of abandonment make Him doubt the rightness of where He was? Did He wonder if He had misunderstood, if He was out of the Father's will? Was He tempted to give up, to lose His faith?

Through it all He remained faithful. Through His childhood, His time in the carpenter shop, the temptation in the wilderness, His early ministry, Gethsemane and Golgotha. Hebrews declares, "He was willing to die a shameful death on the cross because of the joy he knew would be his afterwards . . ." (Heb. 12:2 TLB).

And there were other temptations, many beyond imagining, for ". . . he himself has shared fully in all our experience of temptation . . ." (Heb. 4:15, Phillips). There were the inner doubts and fears, the questions and conflicts. The constant pressure to conform, to fit the popular concept of the Messiah. The temptation to lower the demands of discipleship, to major in miracles, to satisfy the crowd's craze for the spectacular. To use His influence for His own selfish ends. Temptations of the spirit, temptations of the flesh, temptations of the mind—

Yet in it all He remained faithful in love, undeterred from His ordained end. "And being found in human form he humbled himself and became obedient unto death, even death on a cross" (Phil. 2:8).

"Lord,
Your cross is not simply ugly,
it's beautiful!

Not with the pseudo-prettiness
of stained glass and neon,
but beautiful,
with the vibrancy of life
as seen through the reflected light
of the empty tomb!
Yes, it was a place of death,
but it was not a disaster,
it was divine provision.
You were not a helpless captive
but a willing sacrifice.
You became obedient to death,
to the death of the cross.
You refused to be taunted
into coming down
because coming back from the dead
was the ultimate triumph."[2]

TRIUMPHANT IN LOVE

"In June 1815 the English military forces under the Duke of Wellington engaged the forces of Napoleon Bonaparte. All England awaited news of the outcome. It was before the days of fast communication, and watchers were stationed along England's coast to observe the sailing vessels come up the Channel. Any special news would be wigwagged by semaphore to those waiting.

"Knowing the battle was to be fought, the coastal sentries waited for a message of its outcome. Finally a watcher noted a message being waved from a passing boat, 'Wellington defeated. . . .' And then the fog closed in. The words were relayed across England, and the nation was plunged into gloom.

"When the fog cleared again, another sailor on another boat

[2]Richard D. Exley, "The Painted Parable," (Vantage Press, New York, Washington, Atlanta, Hollywood, 1977), p. 21.

waved the same message—this time without interruption: 'Wellington defeated the enemy.' England's sorrow was banished and the entire country went wild with joy."[3]

Late Friday evening the cross appeared to be history's most crushing defeat. ". . . Christ died . . ." and the befogging maze of despair settled in, leaving His handful of faithful followers hopeless. Friday night, Saturday, Saturday night and not the smallest glimmer of hope to brighten the desolate night of their souls. Then early Sunday morning the fog was gone. "He is not here; for he has risen . . ." (Matt. 28:6). The entire meaning could then be clearly seen and understood in the resurrection brightness. ". . . Christ died for our sins . . . he was buried . . . he was raised on the third day [and has become] the first fruits of those who have fallen asleep" (1 Cor. 15:3, 4, 20).

God's daring act of love triumphed. Jesus gave His ". . . back to the smiters . . ." (Isa. 50:6 KJV), voluntarily absorbed all the abuse sinful men heaped upon Him. Sin and darkness did their worst and when they had spent their fury Love was heard praying, ". . . Father, forgive them; for they know not what they do" (Luke 23:34).

". . . He gave up the ghost" (Luke 23:46 KJV). Death claimed its prey. Soldiers abused His lifeless body—thrusting a spear deep in His side. They put His body in a sepulchre, sealed it with a stone, left soldiers under orders to guard it and thought they were finally finished with Him.

But Love would not die, would not stay dead, would not be silent.

"Up from the grave He arose,
With a mighty triumph o'er His foes;
He arose a victor from the dark domain,

[3]Richard E. Orchard, "Our Magnificent Hope," *Advance Magazine*, Volume 4, Number 4 (April, 1968), p. 4.

And He lives forever with His saints to reign.
He arose! He arose!
Hallelujah! Christ arose!''[4]

And love was loosed in the world, and it began changing men. It captured their imagination, excited them, compelled to great sacrifice. They followed His example and took great risks. They were daring in love, faithful in love even to the laying down of their own lives. And like Him they were triumphant. They turned the world upside down! They invaded citadels of sin and paganism and established bastions of righteousness. In a few short years that handful of holy lovers affected the entire known world, and still today His love lives and with a holy contagion affects men for righteousness.

And love's celebration has not really begun. Some day soon we will be part of that great congregation singing love's new song. '' . . . Thou art worthy to take the book, and to open the seals thereof: for thou wast slain, and hast redeemed us to God by thy blood out of every kindred, and tongue, and people, and nation; And hast made us unto our God kings and priests: and we shall reign on earth'' (Rev. 5:9, 10 KJV).

'' . . . The kingdoms of this world are become the kingdoms of our Lord, and of his Christ; and he shall reign for ever and ever'' (Rev. 11:15 KJV). ''And he hath on his vesture, and on his thigh a name written, KING OF KINGS AND LORD OF LORDS'' (Rev. 19:16 KJV).

''For he must reign, till he hath put all enemies under his feet. . . . And when all things shall be subdued unto him, shall the Son also himself be subject unto him that put all things under him, that God may be all in all'' (1 Cor. 15:25, 28 KJV). '' . . . throughout all ages, world without end'' (Eph. 3:21 KJV).

[4]Robert Lowry, ''Christ Arose,'' in ''Hymns of Glorious Praise,'' (Gospel Publishing House, Springfield, Missouri, 1969), p. 105.